Gooseberry Patch

A Country Store In Your Mailbox®

Seasons for Sharing

A Country Store In Your Mailbox®

Gooseberry Patch
600 London Road
P.O. Box 190
Delaware, OH 43015
★

1·800·854·6673
www.gooseberrypatch.com

Do you have a tried & true recipe...

tip, craft or memory that you'd like to see featured in a
Gooseberry Patch book? Visit our web site at
www.gooseberrypatch.com, register and follow the easy steps to
submit your favorite family recipe. Or send them to us at:

Gooseberry Patch
Attn: Book Dept.
P.O. Box 190
Delaware, OH 43015

Don't forget to include the number of servings your recipe makes,
plus your name, street address, phone number and e-mail address.
If we select your recipe, your name will appear right along with
it...and you'll receive a **FREE** copy of the book!

Contents

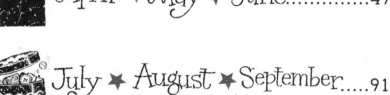
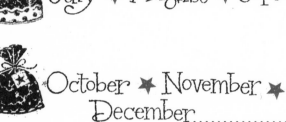

Dedication

Dedicated to everyone who loves making others feel extra special!

Those who bring sunshine into the lives of others, cannot keep it from themselves.
-James M. Barrie

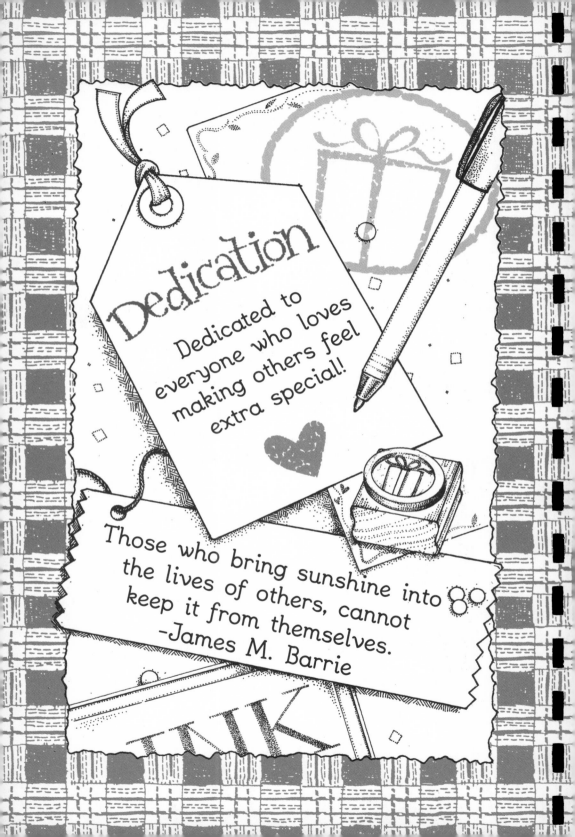

January

February

March

January ⋆ February ⋆ March

Champagne Mustard

A tasty gift sure to delight any hostess when packed along with seasoned toasts and crunchy bagel chips.

2/3 c. champagne vinegar
2/3 c. dry mustard
3 eggs

3/4 c. sugar
1/2 t. dried tarragon or dried
    basil

Whisk vinegar and mustard together; blend in eggs and sugar. Pour into a double boiler; heat and stir until thick. Remove from heat; stir in tarragon or basil. Spoon into an airtight container. Refrigerate up to one week. Makes about 2 cups.

Use a paint marker to write "Happy New Year!" on an ice bucket filled with a jar of Champagne Mustard, breadsticks for dipping, noisemakers and confetti...a ready-made celebration!

Bacon-Tomato Dip

Place a large, festive, backless cookie cutter in the center of a plate and fill with this dip...surround with savory crackers and bright veggies for dipping.

2 c. sour cream
8 slices bacon, crisply cooked
   and crumbled

1 c. cherry tomatoes, chopped
1 T. dried basil

Stir all ingredients together in a mixing bowl; cover with plastic wrap and refrigerate for at least 2 hours. Makes 2-1/2 cups.

Party Nibblers

Fill champagne glasses full of this mix, tie on several long tails of black and silver curling ribbons and set around the room...tasty snacks as well as oh-so-simple party decorations.

1 c. cashews
1 c. peanuts
1 c. bite-size cheese crackers
1 c. bite-size shredded wheat
   cereal squares
1 c. mini pretzels

2 T. grated Parmesan cheese
1/3 c. butter, melted
1 t. Worcestershire sauce
1/2 t. celery salt
1/2 t. garlic powder

Combine the first 6 ingredients in a large mixing bowl; mix well and set aside. Whisk remaining ingredients together in a small bowl; pour over mix, tossing to coat. Spread in an ungreased jelly-roll pan; bake at 350 degrees for 15 to 20 minutes, stirring often. Cool completely; store in an airtight container. Makes 5 cups.

January ★ February ★ March

Banana-Bran Muffin Mix in a Bag

Make up several bags at once...you'll be glad to have them on hand when guests stop by for a New Year's Day visit.

1 c. all-purpose flour
3 T. sugar
2-1/2 t. baking powder

1 t. salt
1 c. whole bran

Combine ingredients in a plastic zipping bag; seal. Attach instructions.

Instructions:

Place mix in a large mixing bowl; add one beaten egg, one cup mashed bananas, 1/4 cup milk and 2 tablespoons oil. Stir until just moistened; fill greased or paper-lined muffin cups 2/3 full with batter. Bake at 400 degrees for 20 to 25 minutes. Makes one dozen.

A festive gift for drop-in friends. Use gold dimensional paint to write "Celebrate!" on a white lunch sack; let dry and add muffin mix. Place a handful of confetti in a 12-inch square of cellophane, gather cellophane around confetti and secure to the top of the sack with a length of wired gold star garland. Just for fun, tuck a noisemaker in the top of the bag!

Confetti Snack Mix

A fruit-filled snack that packs a punch!

2-1/2 qts. popped popcorn
1/2 c. flaked coconut, toasted
1/2 c. chopped almonds, toasted
1/2 c. dried apricots, chopped
1/2 c. dried cherries, chopped

1/4 c. butter
2 T. strawberry jam
2 T. brown sugar, packed
1/2 t. cinnamon

Combine popcorn, coconut, almonds, apricots and cherries in a large
mixing bowl; set aside. Melt butter with jam, brown sugar and
cinnamon in a heavy saucepan over moderate heat; continue heating
to soft-ball stage or 234 to 243 degrees on a candy thermometer. Pour
over popcorn mixture; toss to coat. Makes about 3 quarts.

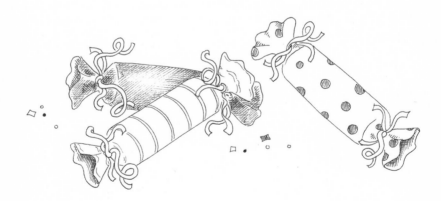

Fill empty cardboard tubes with this fruit mix, then
wrap each tube in colorful tissue paper. Secure open
ends with curling ribbon...what a clever party favor!

January ★ February ★ March

Sand Art Tea in a Jar

A nice little way to celebrate Hot Tea Month in January!

27-oz. container orange drink
   mix
6-oz. pkg. sweetened lemonade
   drink mix

1 c. instant tea
1 c. sugar
1/2 t. ground cloves
1 t. cinnamon

Layer ingredients in order listed in a half-gallon jar with lid, packing each layer firmly. Slide a butter knife gently down the side through all the layers in various places; secure lid. Attach instructions. Makes about 6 cups.

Instructions:

Empty jar contents into a mixing bowl; mix gently and pack back into jar. Add 1/4 cup mix to one cup boiling water; stir to mix. Makes one serving.

Copy, cut & color!

to:

from:

Tea Cookies in a Jar

A cup of tea, a warm plate of cookies...let it snow, let it snow, let it snow!

1-1/2 c. all-purpose flour
1 t. cinnamon
1/2 t. nutmeg
1 t. baking soda
1/2 t. salt

2 c. long-cooking oats,
   uncooked
3/4 c. brown sugar, packed
1/2 c. sugar
3/4 c. raisins

Combine first 5 ingredients together; layer in a one-quart, wide-mouth jar. Pack firmly; layer remaining ingredients except raisins in order listed, packing each layer. Spoon raisins into a plastic zipping bag. Secure lid; tie on raisins and instructions.

Instructions:

Empty mix and raisins into a large mixing bowl; toss gently to blend. Add 3/4 cup softened butter, one beaten egg and one teaspoon vanilla extract; mix well. Shape into one-inch balls; arrange 2 inches apart on parchment paper-lined baking sheets. Bake at 350 degrees for 10 to 12 minutes; cool on baking sheets for 5 minutes. Remove to wire racks to cool completely. Makes 3 dozen.

As an extra treat, bake a batch of Tea Cookies to give along with this mix. Stack inside a dainty teacup and tie with ribbon...a welcome gift on a chilly day!

"Good Morning!" Mix

So handy...so good!

3 c. all-purpose flour	2 t. salt
1 c. brown sugar, packed	1-1/2 c. shortening
1/2 c. sugar	3 c. quick-cooking oats,
3-1/2 t. baking powder	uncooked

Combine first 5 ingredients; cut in shortening with a pastry cutter until fine crumbs form. Stir in oats; store in an airtight container in a cool dry place up to 6 months. Attach instructions. Makes about 8 cups.

Oat Pancakes:

Combine 1-1/2 cups "Good Morning!" Mix, one beaten egg and one cup water; mix well. Set aside for 5 minutes. Pour by 1/4 cupfuls onto a hot, greased griddle; turn when bubbles form along the edge. Heat until golden on both sides. Makes 10 servings.

Oat Muffins:

Combine 3 cups "Good Morning!" Mix, one beaten egg and 2/3 cup milk; mix well. Fill paper-lined muffin cups 2/3 full with batter; bake at 400 degrees for 15 to 20 minutes. Cool in pan for 5 minutes before removing to wire rack to cool completely. Makes one dozen.

Friendship Bars in a Jar

*Tie a wooden spoon to the jar for a welcome
"glad you're my friend" treat!*

1/2 c. pecan pieces
1 c. butterscotch chips
1 c. chocolate chips

1 c. flaked coconut
1-1/2 c. graham cracker crumbs

Layer ingredients in the order listed in a one-quart, wide-mouth jar;
pack tightly after each addition. Secure lid; tie on instructions.

Instructions:

Melt 1/2 cup butter; pour into a mixing bowl. Carefully spoon in
graham cracker crumbs from jar mix; toss gently. Pat mixture evenly
in bottom of an ungreased 13"x9" baking pan; sprinkle with remaining
ingredients, spreading evenly. Pour 14-ounce can sweetened
condensed milk on top; bake at 350 degrees for 30 minutes. Cool;
cut into squares to serve. Makes 3 dozen.

For gift-giving, this jar of
Friendship Bars will fit
nicely into a berry basket.
Tie on a colorful pair of
woolly mittens along with
a tag that reads
"Friendship warms
the heart."

friendship
warms ♥
the heart

January ★ February ★ March

Bottle au Bubble Bath

Grab your favorite paperback book, fill up the tub, add some bubble bath and enjoy January 8th...National Bubble Bath Day!

2 c. unscented soap flakes or grated soap
1 gal. water

1/3 c. glycerin, divided
2 c. unscented baby shampoo
6 to 12 drops essential oil

Combine soap, water and 2 tablespoons glycerin in a saucepan; heat over low heat, stirring occasionally, until soap dissolves. Add 2 cups mixture to a large mixing bowl; store remaining mixture in an airtight container for later use. Stir in remaining glycerin, shampoo and essential oil. Pour into a one-quart container with a lid; store at room temperature. Makes about 2-1/2 cups.

This bubble bath is so pretty poured into an old-fashioned glass bottle with a cork stopper. Give the bottle some sparkle by stringing jewel-toned beads on wire and carefully wrapping around the bottleneck.

Surprise Bubble Bath Bars

Simply dissolve under running water for a bathtub brimming with bubbles.

1 env. unflavored gelatin mix
3/4 c. boiling water
1/2 c. clear liquid soap
10 drops essential oil

1/2-inch toys, flowers or plastic
   figures
ice cube tray

Stir gelatin into water until dissolved; gradually mix in liquid soap and essential oil. Pour 1/4 inch mixture into each section of the ice cube tray that has been coated with non-stick vegetable spray; carefully arrange one object in each cube. Pour remaining mixture on top to cover each object; refrigerate until firm, 3 to 5 hours. Makes about 6.

Rose-Scented Bath Salts

So relaxing...so soothing...so simple!

2 c. Epsom salt
1 c. sea salt
20 drops rose essential oil

1 T. glycerin
2 to 3 drops red food coloring

Mix salts together in a large plastic zipping bag; shake to combine. Add essential oil and glycerin; shake to mix. Add food coloring, drop by drop, until desired tint is achieved shaking well between drops. Pour into a 3-cup container; secure lid. Makes 3 cups.

January ★ February ★ March

Onion Bread Mix in a Jar

This recipe can also be baked in a bread machine, just follow the manufacturer's instructions for "white" bread.

1/4 c. dried, minced onion
3-1/3 c. bread flour
2 T. sugar
1 T. powdered milk

1-1/2 t. salt
1/2 t. dried sage
1 pkg. active dry yeast

Place dried, minced onion in a small plastic zipping bag and set aside. Combine flour, sugar, powdered milk, salt and sage; spoon into a one-quart, wide-mouth jar. Tuck the plastic zipping bag and package of yeast on top; secure lid. Attach instructions.

Instructions:

Sprinkle yeast over 1-1/8 cups of 105 to 110-degree water; set aside until foamy. Place flour mixture in a large mixing bowl; add contents of plastic zipping bag. Blend in yeast mixture and one tablespoon olive oil; mix until smooth. Knead 5 minutes; place dough in a greased mixing bowl, turning once to coat both sides. Cover with plastic wrap and set aside to rise until double in bulk; punch down. Form dough into a loaf; place in a greased 9"x5" loaf pan. Cover and let rise until double. Bake at 350 degrees until golden, about 30 minutes. Makes 8 servings.

To make a snowman bag, fold down the top of a white lunch sack; round the edges with scissors. Add eyes and a mouth using a black pen, and glue on an orange craft foam nose. Top him off with an infant-size hat!

16

A-B-C Wintertime Soup Mix

A warm, hearty helping will be greeted with cheers, especially following an afternoon of sledding.

14-oz. pkg. dried split green
   peas
1-1/2 c. long-cooking brown
   rice, uncooked

14-oz. pkg. alphabet macaroni
12-oz. pkg. pearled barley
12-oz. pkg. dried lentils
4 c. dried, minced onion

Combine all ingredients in a large airtight container; shake to mix. Store in a cool, dry place for up to 6 months. Shake well before using. Attach instructions. Makes about 12-1/2 cups.

Instructions:

6 c. water
1-1/2 T. garlic salt
2 carrots, sliced
2 stalks celery, sliced
1-1/2 c. cabbage, shredded

2 15-oz. cans tomato sauce
24-oz. can cocktail vegetable
   juice
1 lb. ground beef, browned

Place water, garlic salt and 1-1/2 cups A-B-C Wintertime Soup Mix in a large Dutch oven; bring to a boil. Reduce heat; simmer, covered, for 1-1/2 hours. Add remaining ingredients; simmer until vegetables are tender, about 20 minutes. Makes 6 to 8 servings.

A white toddler-size fleece hat makes a sweet topper for this mix. Stitch on buttons for eyes and a mouth, then add a bright orange pom-pom for a nose!

January ✦ February ✦ March

Mocha-Almond Popcorn

A crispy-crunchy snack mix that's perfect for movie night.

1/2 c. brewed coffee
1/2 c. corn syrup
1/4 c. butter
1 c. brown sugar, packed

1 T. baking cocoa
2-1/2 qts. popped popcorn
1 c. chopped almonds, toasted

Combine first 5 ingredients in a heavy saucepan; heat to soft-crack stage, or 270 to 289 degrees on a candy thermometer. Remove from heat; set aside. Mix popcorn and almonds together in a large mixing bowl; pour brown sugar mixture on top, tossing to coat. Makes 10 to 12 cups.

Know someone who loves the movies? Delight them with Mocha-Almond Popcorn served inside a bucket decoupaged with magazine cut-outs of their favorite stars. Or for another spin, add vintage postcards, stickers or the Sunday comics!

Double Fudge, Double Good Brownie Mix

Warming up is easy on a frosty winter's day with a plate of these yummy brownies.

2 c. sugar
1 c. baking cocoa
1 c. all-purpose flour

1 c. chopped pecans
1 c. chocolate chips

Combine ingredients; store in an airtight container. Attach instructions.

Instructions:

Cream one cup softened butter in a large mixing bowl; add 4 eggs, one at a time, mixing well after each addition. Blend in brownie mix; mix until smooth. Spread in a greased 13"x9" baking pan; bake at 325 degrees for 40 to 50 minutes. Cool and cut into squares to serve. Makes 2 dozen.

Tuck several packages of this double-delicious brownie mix into a long woolen stocking. Or better yet, a pair of stockings...a toasty gift for a frosty winter morn!

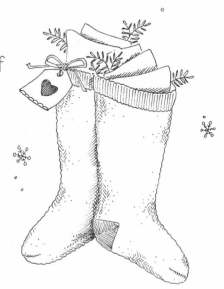

January ★ February ★ March

Creamy Sweet Mustard Sauce

A welcome surprise anyone would enjoy in front of a glowing fire.

2 c. shredded Cheddar cheese
1 c. shredded sharp Cheddar
   cheese
2 3-oz. pkgs. cream cheese,
   softened

2 T. honey
2 T. dill weed
1 T. onion, minced
1 T. dry mustard
1 t. dried chives

Place all ingredients in a food processor; blend until smooth and creamy. Spoon into an airtight container; refrigerate overnight. Makes 2-1/3 cups.

Creamy Sweet Mustard Sauce can be spooned into a vintage milk bottle and then set inside a wooden milk carrier for gift-giving. Fill the rest of the carrier with crackers, bread sticks, bagel chips...lots of good snacks for dipping!

Wintry Gift Crate

Simply save the little crates that clementines and tangelos are often boxed in at the grocer…they're the perfect size for a great crate!

snowman stencil
stencil brush
14"x8" wooden crate
white, black and orange acrylic
   paints

silver permanent felt-tip marker
green raffia
checked dishtowel

Stencil 3 to 5 snowmen along the longer sides of the crate with white paint; add black top hats, eyes and mouths and orange noses. Draw on snowflakes using silver pen; tie a big raffia bow on one end. Let dry; line crate with dishtowel. Fill with a crock of cheese spread and an assortment of crackers.

Snowmen stencilled along the side of a wooden crate
make a cheery carry-all for any wintry treat!

January ★ February ★ March

Brocomole Dip

Use broccoli instead of avocado in this traditional guacamole dish for a little more "broc" than "guac"...always a hit at Super Bowl parties.

2 c. broccoli, chopped
1/4 c. sour cream
3 T. onion, chopped

1 T. mayonnaise
juice of one lemon
1/2 t. chili powder

Boil broccoli until crisp-tender; drain and chill. Place in a food processor; add remaining ingredients. Blend until smooth; spread into a serving bowl. Cover with plastic wrap and refrigerate until chilled. Makes about 2-1/2 cups.

Buffalo Wing-Style Popcorn Mix

Simply turn up the heat by sprinkling with cayenne pepper.

2-1/2 qts. popped popcorn
2 c. corn chips, coarsely broken
1 c. dry-roasted peanuts
1/4 c. butter

2 T. hot pepper sauce
1 t. celery seed
1/4 t. garlic salt

Place 2 cups popcorn to the side; combine remaining popcorn, corn chips and peanuts in a large mixing bowl. Set aside. Melt butter with hot pepper sauce, celery seed and garlic salt in a small saucepan; pour over popcorn mixture, tossing to coat. Spread in an ungreased jelly-roll pan; bake at 350 degrees for 10 minutes. Place back into large mixing bowl; mix in reserved popcorn. Store in airtight container. Makes about 12 cups.

Baked Potato Skins Seasoning Mix

A fun mix for that potato-lover...tie it on a bag of russet potatoes for an even more spud-tacular Super Bowl gift!

1 t. salt
1/2 t. pepper
1-1/2 t. chili powder

1-1/2 t. curry powder
1-1/2 t. ground coriander

Combine all ingredients in a small airtight jar with a shaker lid; attach instructions.

Instructions:

Bake 4 potatoes; scoop out potato pulp, leaving skins with 1/4-inch thick potato shell. Reserve potato pulp for use in another recipe. Slice each potato half lengthwise into 3 sections; coat with olive oil. Arrange on an ungreased baking sheet; sprinkle Baked Potato Skins Seasoning Mix on top. Bake until golden and crispy, about 15 additional minutes. Serve warm. Makes 2 dozen.

Why not give a Baked Potato Kit to a favorite friend? Fold the top edges of a brown paper grocery bag over to make a cuff, then line bag inside and out with kitchen towels. Load up the bag with potatoes, salsa, sour cream, butter, bacon bits and Baked Potato Skins Seasoning Mix...a sure winner!

January ★ February ★ March

Have-on-Hand Cherry Pie Filling

*February is National Pie Month...celebrate with
a fresh-baked cherry pie.*

1/2 gal. water
3-1/3 c. cherries, pitted and
    stemmed
1 c. sugar
1/4 c. plus 1 T. instant modified
    food starch
1-1/3 c. cold water

1/8 t. cinnamon
1/2 t. almond extract
6 drops red food coloring
1 T. plus 1 t. lemon juice
1-quart, wide-mouth canning jar
    and lid, sterilized

Bring water to a boil in a large saucepan; add cherries and return to a
boil. Boil for one minute; drain. Cover hot cherries; set pan aside. Place
sugar and food starch in a large saucepan; add cold water, cinnamon,
extract and food coloring. Heat over high heat until mixture thickens
and begins to boil; stir constantly. Add lemon juice and cherries; stir
and boil for one minute. Pour into hot jar leaving a one-inch
headspace; wipe rim. Secure lid and ring; process in a boiling water
bath for 30 minutes. Makes one quart.

For a fun retro look, give a quart jar of
Have-on-Hand Cherry Pie Filling inside a cheery
cherry canister!

Wow 'Em with Blueberry Pie

Happy Presidents' Day! We cannot tell a lie...sometimes we just like blueberry better than cherry pie!

3 T. cornstarch
3 T. plus 2 t. water
1 T. lemon juice
2/3 c. plus 1-1/2 T. sugar,
   divided

1/4 t. cinnamon
8 c. blueberries, stemmed,
   rinsed and drained
2 10-inch deep-dish pie crusts
1 egg white

Combine cornstarch, 3 tablespoons water, lemon juice, 2/3 cup sugar and cinnamon in a large mixing bowl; add blueberries, tossing gently to mix. Set aside. Place one pie crust into a deep-dish pie plate; fill with blueberry mixture. Roll out remaining pie crust and arrange on top; pinch and flute edges. Vent top crust; set aside. Whisk remaining water and egg white; brush on crust. Sprinkle with remaining sugar; place on a baking sheet. Bake at 375 degrees until golden and filling is bubbly, about one to 1-1/4 hours, covering edges with aluminum foil if necessary during baking to prevent browning. Cool on a wire rack. Makes 8 to 10 servings.

Celebrate Great American Pie Month in February by tucking a mini flag in the center of this delicious pie.

January ★ February ★ March

Oriental Snack Mix

*The combination of ingredients in this mix turn simple popcorn
into a tasty treat that's impossible to stop snacking on!*

3 T. butter
3 T. creamy peanut butter
2 t. soy sauce

1 clove garlic, minced
2-1/2 qts. popped popcorn
2 c. chow mein noodles

Melt butter and peanut butter with soy sauce and garlic in a small
saucepan over medium-low heat; stir until smooth. Set aside.
Combine popcorn and chow mein noodles; drizzle with peanut butter
mixture. Toss to coat; spread on an ungreased jelly-roll pan. Bake at
300 degrees for 10 to 15 minutes, stirring after 5 minutes; cool and
store in an airtight container. Makes about 12 cups.

Celebrate the Chinese New Year (based on the first full
moon, it always falls between January 21 and
February 21) by sharing snack mixes served in
Chinese food take-out containers...don't forget to tie
on a fortune cookie!

Spicy Beijing Pecans

*Stir up Chinese New Year celebrations with these
hot & spicy pecans.*

1-1/2 qts. water
12-oz. pkg. pecan halves
1/4 c. corn syrup
2-1/2 T. soy sauce

1-1/2 t. onion powder
1 t. garlic powder
1/2 t. cayenne pepper

Bring water to a boil in a large saucepan; add pecans and boil for
2 minutes. Drain; set aside. Combine remaining ingredients in a large
saucepan; heat over medium-high heat until mixture boils, stirring
constantly. Add pecans; heat and stir until pecans absorb sauce, about
3 to 4 minutes. Remove from heat; spread in a single layer in a
greased jelly-roll pan. Bake at 250 degrees for 40 minutes, stirring and
turning pecans over every 15 minutes. Cool completely. Store in an
airtight container. Makes about 3 cups.

A brightly painted paper maché box is ideal for
holding all the goodies needed for celebrating the
Chinese New Year...fortune cookies, a box of
green tea, chopsticks, a favorite stir-fry recipe and
Spicy Beijing Pecans for munching on!

Be-My-Sweetie Cupcakes

Sprinkle with conversation hearts, little red cinnamon candies or mini red, white and pink jellybeans for a special Valentine's Day treat.

18-1/2 oz. pkg. white cake mix
1-1/3 c. water
3 egg whites
2 T. butter, melted
1/2 t. peppermint extract

3 to 4 drops red food coloring
16-oz. container vanilla frosting
16 to 20 red & white peppermint
    candies, crushed

Blend the first 6 ingredients together on low speed of an electric mixer for 30 seconds; increase speed to medium and blend 2 additional minutes. Spoon batter into paper-lined muffin cups until 3/4 full; bake at 350 degrees for 20 to 24 minutes or until a toothpick inserted in the center removes clean. Cool on wire racks 10 minutes; remove cupcakes to wire racks to cool completely. Frost; sprinkle with candies. Makes 2-1/2 dozen.

A plate of Be-My-Sweetie Cupcakes would make any heart go pitter-pat! Give them inside a decorated mailbox for a heartfelt Valentine's Day gift...add a postcard that says "Special Delivery."

BE MINE

LOVE

Special Delivery

White Fudge Hearts

For a sweet finish, pipe a letter using melted chocolate on each candy to spell out a heartfelt message.

1-1/2 c. milk
3-1/2 c. sugar

8 T. butter, thinly sliced
Garnish: colored fine sugar

Pour milk into a 2-quart heavy saucepan; stir in sugar and butter. Heat over medium heat, stirring constantly, until sugar dissolves and butter melts; increase heat to medium-high. Bring mixture to a boil; cover and let boil 2 minutes. Uncover; reduce heat to medium-low. Do not stir; heat mixture to the soft-ball stage, or 234 to 243 degrees on a candy thermometer, 15 to 20 minutes. Remove pan from heat; set in an ice bath for 5 minutes. Set mixture aside at room temperature until thermometer registers 122 degrees without stirring, about 40 minutes. Stir with a wooden spoon until thick and creamy, about 2 to 5 minutes; spread into a greased 9"x9" baking pan. Sprinkle with fine sugar; cool completely, 2 to 3 hours. Cut with one-inch greased heart-shaped cookie cutters; wrap individually in plastic wrap and store in an airtight container. Makes about 4 dozen.

It's easy to make the prettiest sweetheart bag in minutes. Cut a heart shape from the front of a pink or red gift bag. Center clear cellophane inside the bag over the heart opening; glue in place. Fill the bag with White Fudge Hearts and add a silk ribbon bow to the bag handles.

January ★ February ★ March

Tickled-Pink Drink

An all-occasion pretty-in-pink drink!

1/2 c. milk
1/2 c. vanilla yogurt
1 c. orange juice
10-oz. pkg. frozen strawberries,
    thawed

1 t. almond extract
Garnish: one orange, sliced into
    thin wedges

Place all ingredients except orange wedges into a blender; cover and blend until smooth, 40 to 50 seconds. Pour into serving glasses; garnish each with an orange wedge. Makes 4 to 6 servings.

Search flea markets and tag sales for tall
Depression-era tumblers. Delicate patterns
with names like Rose of Sharon, Cabbage Rose and
Iris are oh-so pretty when filled
with Tickled-Pink Drink.

Pe-tea Fours

*Wrap individually in brightly colored cellophane for
tea party or shower favors.*

18-1/2 oz. pkg. white cake mix
1/2 t. almond extract

Garnish: candy or frosting
flowers

Prepare cake mix according to package directions; add almond
extract, blending well. Spread evenly into 2 greased and floured
9"x9" baking pans; bake at 350 degrees for 20 to 30 minutes or until
a toothpick inserted in the center removes clean. Cool on wire racks for
10 minutes; remove from pans and cool completely. Trim edges from
cakes; slice each cake into 24 squares. Arrange on a wire rack that is
placed in a jelly-roll pan. Spoon icing over cake squares; repeat until
each piece is coated, scraping and reheating icing from jelly-roll pan.
Garnish each with a flower. Makes 4 dozen.

Icing:

3 c. sugar
1/4 t. cream of tartar
1-1/2 c. water

1 c. powdered sugar
1 t. almond extract
3 drops desired food coloring

Combine sugar, cream of tartar and water in a 3-quart saucepan; heat
over medium heat until mixture comes to a full boil, about 12 to
14 minutes, stirring occasionally. Cover; boil for 3 minutes. Uncover;
heat until mixture reaches 226 degrees on a candy thermometer.
Remove from heat; set aside without stirring until mixture registers
110 degrees. Stir in remaining ingredients. Use immediately; reheat
over low heat to regain pouring consistency, if necessary.

January ★ February ★ March

Me-yum, Meow Mix

Love Your Pet Day falls on February 20...let's treat all those friendly critters that keep us cozy!

1/2 c. canned mackerel, drained
1 c. whole-grain bread crumbs
1 T. oil

1 egg, beaten
1/2 t. brewer's yeast

Mash mackerel in a medium mixing bowl with a fork; add remaining ingredients, mixing well. Drop by 1/4 teaspoonfuls onto a greased baking sheet; bake at 350 degrees for 8 minutes. Cool to room temperature; store in an airtight container. Makes about 4 dozen.

Bird Treats in a Jar

Oh-so tweet!

1 c. quick-cooking oats,
    uncooked
1/3 c. brown sugar, packed
3/4 c. whole sunflower seeds

1 c. millet birdseed
3/4 c. cornmeal
3/4 c. all-purpose flour

Layer the first 4 ingredients in the order listed in a one-quart, wide-mouth jar; set aside. Combine cornmeal and flour; layer on top, packing down firmly. Secure lid; attach instructions.

Instructions:

Place mix in a medium mixing bowl; add one cup creamy peanut butter and 1/2 cup water, mixing well. Spread in an ungreased 13"x9" baking pan; score into 4"x2" bars. Bake at 250 degrees for 20 minutes. Set aside to cool; cut into bars. Makes one dozen.

Bow-Wow-Good Biscuits Mix

A perfect surprise for any pet lover!

1 c. all-purpose flour
1 c. whole-wheat flour
1/2 c. cornmeal
1/2 c. powdered milk

1 t. brown sugar, packed
1 t. garlic powder
1/4 t. salt

Combine all ingredients in a mixing bowl; toss to combine. Place in a plastic zipping bag; seal. Attach instructions.

Instructions:

Place mix in a medium mixing bowl; stir in one beaten egg, 1/2 cup shredded Cheddar cheese, 1/4 cup grated Parmesan cheese, 1/3 cup hot chicken or beef broth. Mix well; knead 8 to 10 times on a lightly floured surface. Roll out to 1/2-inch thickness; cut out with a dog bone-shaped cookie cutter. Arrange on ungreased baking sheets; bake at 250 degrees for one hour. Cool on pan for one minute; transfer to wire racks to cool completely. Makes one to 1-1/2 dozen.

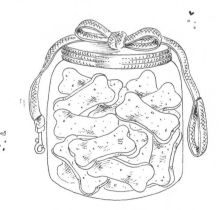

Treat a favorite four-legged friend to a pantry jar filled with Bow-Wow-Good Biscuits, then top off the jar with a brand new leash tied up in a bow!

January ★ February ★ March

Cajun Spice Seasoning in a Jar

A Mardi gras kitchen necessity for any potato, egg or meat dish.

3/4 c. salt
1/4 c. cayenne pepper
2 T. white pepper
2 T. black pepper

2 T. paprika
2 T. onion powder
2 T. garlic powder
1 t. onion salt

Combine ingredients; spoon into a one-pint container with lid. Store in a cool, dry cupboard. Makes 1-1/2 cups.

Louisiana Mustard

Tuck in a basket with plenty of salami and crackers.

2-oz. pkg. dry mustard
1 T. all-purpose flour
1/4 c. cold water
3 T. white wine vinegar
1 T. honey
1 clove garlic, minced

1 T. red pepper flakes
1-1/2 t. pepper
1 t. ground cumin
1 t. dried thyme
1 t. paprika

Combine mustard and flour; gradually stir in water. Let stand 15 minutes; whisk in remaining ingredients. Store in an airtight container in the refrigerator up to 2 weeks.

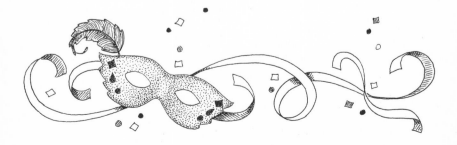

Jambalaya Mix

When sharing the instructions, jot down a couple different Jambalaya options…maybe a mixture of ham & sausage or sausage & shrimp.

1 c. long-cooking rice, uncooked
1 T. dried, minced onion
1 T. green pepper flakes
1 T. dried parsley
1 bay leaf

2 t. beef bouillon granules
1/2 t. garlic powder
1/2 t. dried thyme
1/2 t. cayenne pepper

Combine all ingredients; place in a one-gallon plastic zipping bag. Seal securely; attach instructions.

Instructions:

Combine mix with 3 cups water in a large stockpot; bring to a boil. Reduce heat; add 1/2 cup diced ham and an 8-ounce can tomato sauce. Simmer for 20 minutes. Stir in 1/2 cup cooked shrimp; heat 5 additional minutes. Remove from heat; discard bay leaf before serving. Makes 8 cups.

No Mardi Gras basket is complete without this Jambalaya Mix...and don't forget to fill the basket with plenty of colorful beads, a jar of hot pepper sauce, a bag of red beans & rice, pralines and a feathered Mardi Gras mask!

January ★ February ★ March

Peanut Butter S'mores

National Peanut Butter Day is January 24th, National Peanut Butter Month is March, but Peanut Butter Lover's Month is November…it's best to just keep these on hand all year 'round!

1-1/2 c. all-purpose flour
1/2 t. baking powder
1/2 t. baking soda
1/4 t. salt
1/2 c. butter, softened
1/2 c. sugar
1/2 c. brown sugar, packed

1/2 c. creamy peanut butter
1 egg
1-1/2 t. vanilla extract
1/2 c. chopped peanuts
4 1-1/2 oz. milk chocolate
    candy bars
16 marshmallows

Combine first 4 ingredients in a small mixing bowl; set aside. Cream butter and sugars in a large mixing bowl until light and fluffy; blend in peanut butter, egg and vanilla. Gradually blend in flour mixture; fold in peanuts. Roll dough into one-inch balls; arrange 2 inches apart on ungreased baking sheets. Flatten with tines of a fork, forming a criss-cross pattern; bake at 350 degrees for 12 to 14 minutes. Cool on baking sheets for 2 minutes; remove to wire rack to cool completely. To assemble, break each candy bar into 4 sections. Place one section on flat side of one cookie; place on a microwave-safe plate. Top with one marshmallow; heat on high setting 10 to 12 seconds or until marshmallow is puffy. Immediately top with another cookie, flat-side down; press lightly to spread marshmallow to edges. Set aside to cool completely. Repeat with remaining cookies. Makes about 16.

Line a tin pail with gingham wax paper and fill with Peanut Butter S'mores. Tie a big napkin to the pail handle for wiping chins covered in gooey chocolate!

Peanut Butter Lover's Muffin Mix in a Bag

*Tuck into a basket with a jar of jam to enjoy along with these
moist, delicious muffins.*

2 c. all-purpose flour   2-1/2 t. baking powder
1/2 c. sugar   1 t. salt

Combine all ingredients; place in a plastic zipping bag. Seal;
attach instructions.

Instructions:

Place mix in a large mixing bowl; cut in 1/2 cup crunchy peanut butter
and 2 tablespoons butter with a pastry cutter until coarse crumbs
form. Stir in 3/4 cup milk and 2 beaten eggs until just moistened; fill
greased or paper-lined muffin cups 2/3 full. Bake at 400 degrees for
15 to 18 minutes. Makes 1-1/2 to 2 dozen.

It's a snap to make a
fabric-covered gift bag, just cut
fabric to the same size as the
front and back of a lunch bag.
Follow manufacturer's directions
to fuse paper-backed fusible web
to fabric. Remove paper backing,
center and fuse fabric to both
sides of bag. Set mix inside bag
and fold top of bag over. Hot
glue 2 buttons to bag and tie
closed with cotton string.

January ★ February ★ March

Blueberry Pancake Mix in a Jar

Now here's a day to flip over...National Pancake Day is March 4th!

1 c. all-purpose flour
1/3 c. cornmeal
2 T. sugar
1-1/2 T. baking powder

1/2 t. baking soda
1/2 t. salt
1 c. blueberries

Combine all ingredients except blueberries; spoon into a one-pint jar. Secure lid. Place blueberries in a plastic container or plastic zipping bag; tie onto jar. Attach instructions.

Instructions:

Whisk 1-1/3 cups buttermilk, one beaten egg and 2 tablespoons oil together; add pancake mix, stirring until just moistened. Gently fold in blueberries. Pour by 1/4 cupfuls on a hot, greased griddle; heat until bubbles form along the edges. Turn and heat until golden on both sides. Makes one dozen.

A gift in a jiffy! Line a spatterware bowl with homespun, set Blueberry Pancake Mix inside, add a pitcher of syrup, crock of butter, whisk and spatula.

Lunch Lady Cookies in a Jar

National School Breakfast Week is the first week in March…why not treat your "lunch ladies" to a special gift.

1-1/4 c. sugar
1/2 t. salt

2-1/2 c. flaked coconut
1-1/2 c. corn flake cereal

Pack sugar and salt in a one-quart, wide-mouth jar; add coconut, packing firmly. Spoon in cereal; pack but do not crush. Secure lid; attach instructions.

Instructions:

Whisk 3 egg whites until stiff; add 1/2 teaspoon vanilla extract. Stir in cookie mix; drop dough by teaspoonfuls 2 inches apart onto ungreased baking sheets. Bake at 325 degrees for 15 minutes. Makes 3 to 4 dozen.

Any lunch lady will love this cookie mix when it's given in a canvas lunch bag decorated using rubber stamps of the alphabet, pencils, crayons and school buses!

Chocolatey Chocolate Chip Cookies in a Jar

The first week in March is Chocolate Chip Cookie Week...need we say more?

1-3/4 c. all-purpose flour
1 t. baking powder
1 t. baking soda
1/2 t. salt
3/4 c. brown sugar, packed

1/2 c. sugar
1/4 c. baking cocoa
1/2 c. chopped pecans
1 c. semi-sweet chocolate chips

Combine flour, baking powder, baking soda and salt; layer in a one-quart, wide-mouth jar, packing down firmly. Add brown sugar, sugar and cocoa, packing firmly between layers; secure lid. Place pecans and chocolate chips in a plastic zipping bag; attach to the jar along with instructions.

Instructions:

Empty mix and bag contents into a large mixing bowl; add 3/4 cup softened butter, one beaten egg and 1-1/2 teaspoons vanilla extract. Mix well; shape into one-inch balls. Arrange 2 inches apart on a parchment paper-lined baking sheet; bake at 350 degrees for 12 to 14 minutes. Cool on baking sheet 5 minutes; remove to wire racks to cool completely. Makes about 3 dozen.

Pack these yummy cookies up in a toy sailboat and ship them off to your best mate!

Jumbo Chocolate Chip-Walnut Cookies

The bigger the scoop, the better!

2-1/3 c. all-purpose flour
1 t. baking soda
1/2 t. salt
1 c. butter, softened
1 c. brown sugar, packed

3/4 c. sugar
2 eggs
1-1/2 t. almond extract
2 c. semi-sweet chocolate chips
1 c. chopped walnuts

Mix flour, baking soda and salt together in a medium mixing bowl; set aside. Cream butter with sugars until light and fluffy; blend in eggs, one at a time, blending well after each addition. Add extract; gradually mix in flour mixture. Stir in chocolate chips and walnuts with a wooden spoon; drop by heaping tablespoonfuls 4 inches apart onto ungreased baking sheets. Bake at 375 degrees until golden, about 9 to 12 minutes; cool 2 to 3 minutes on baking sheets and then remove to wire rack to cool completely. Makes about 5 dozen.

Give friends a jumbo cookie tucked inside a glassine candy bag...what could be better?

January ★ February ★ March

Blarney Stone Cookies in a Jar

So easy even the littlest leprechaun can help make these!

1 c. sugar
3/4 c. golden raisins
1-1/4 c. salted peanuts

1-3/4 c. all-purpose flour
1 t. baking soda
1 t. allspice

Layer sugar, raisins and peanuts in a one-quart, wide-mouth jar, packing firmly between layers; set aside. Combine remaining ingredients in a mixing bowl; gradually add to jar, packing firmly. Secure lid; attach instructions.

Instructions:

Place cookie mix in a large mixing bowl; toss gently to mix. Add 1/4 cup softened butter, 2 beaten eggs and 1-1/2 teaspoons vanilla extract. Mix well; shape dough into one-inch balls and arrange 2 inches apart on a greased baking sheet. Bake at 375 degrees for 9 to 12 minutes. Cool on baking sheet for 5 minutes; remove to wire rack to cool completely. Makes about 3-1/2 dozen.

A black bucket piled high with these peanutty cookies will be a pot-of-gold to anyone lucky enough to receive them! Top off this yummy treasure with a big green bow and clover-shaped tag.

Irish Soda Bread

A sweet recipe enough for 2 loaves...one to share, one to enjoy!

4 c. all-purpose flour
1 c. sugar
1 t. baking soda
2 t. baking powder
1/2 t. salt

3 eggs
2 c. sour cream
1 c. raisins
1 T. caraway seed

Blend the first 5 ingredients together in a large mixing bowl; add eggs and sour cream, mixing until just moistened. Fold in raisins; spread batter evenly into 2 greased 8"x4" loaf pans. Sprinkle with caraway seed; bake at 325 degrees for one hour. Makes 2 loaves.

Set a loaf of Irish Soda Bread inside a green fabric gift bag...toss some chocolate gold coins for little leprechauns to enjoy!

January ★ February ★ March

Fresh Herb Rice

*Try these other spring herbs for variety…oregano, parsley, thyme,
verbena or lemon thyme.*

4 c. long-grain white rice,
   uncooked
1/3 c. lemon zest

1/4 c. chicken bouillon granules
2 T. dried dill
1 T. dried chives

Combine all ingredients; spoon into a plastic zipping bag. Seal; attach
instructions. Store in a cool, dry place; use within 4 months. Makes
about 4-3/4 cups.

Instructions:

Bring 2 cups water and one tablespoon butter to a simmer; stir in one
cup rice mix. Cover and simmer until liquid is absorbed, about 15 to
20 minutes. Makes 4 to 6 servings.

A vintage canning jar makes a pretty gift when filled
with this herbal rice mix. Set the jar inside a garden
trug along with lots of little potted herb plants.

Springtime Pea Soup Mix

One taste of this soup will remind you of all the fresh veggies just waiting to sprout...Happy 1st day of Spring, March 20!

16-oz. pkg. split green peas
16-oz. pkg. dried lentils
16-oz. pkg. pearled barley
2 c. elbow macaroni, uncooked
1 c. dried, minced onion

1/2 c. celery flakes
1/2 c. dried parsley
2 t. white pepper
1-1/2 t. dried thyme

Combine all ingredients together; spoon into a jar with a tight fitting lid. Attach instructions. Makes 10 cups.

Instructions:

Combine one cup soup mix with 4 cups seasoned chicken broth; add one cup cooked chicken, if desired. Bring to a boil; reduce heat and simmer until peas are tender, about 45 to 60 minutes. Serves 4.

Spring has sprung! Use decoupage medium to attach a vintage-style pea seed packet to the front of a quart jar filled with Springtime Pea Soup Mix...what pretty packaging!

January ★ February ★ March

Teacup Candles

Here's what to do with all those flea market teacup & saucer finds!

teacups   waxed wicks
empty coffee can   saucers
creamy wax in a favorite scent

Pour hot water into teacups to warm them while wax is melting. Pinch one edge of the coffee can to make a spout for easy pouring of hot wax. Drop wax into the coffee can, setting the can in a pan of water on the stove to create a double-boiler. When wax is thoroughly melted, remove from heat; set aside. Pour hot water out of teacups; dry thoroughly. Set a waxed wick inside each teacup; carefully pour wax into teacups. Set aside until a soft covering appears on top of the wax, about two or three minutes. Place teacups on saucers; trim wick as desired.

For other great candle containers, scout flea markets for sugar jars, creamers and small serving bowls. To add a decorative spoon to a Teacup Candle, simply lay it on the saucer, securing with a dab of hot wax.

Lucky Me!

...to have a friend like you!

Make a copy of these little tags & tie them on for extra-special gifts!

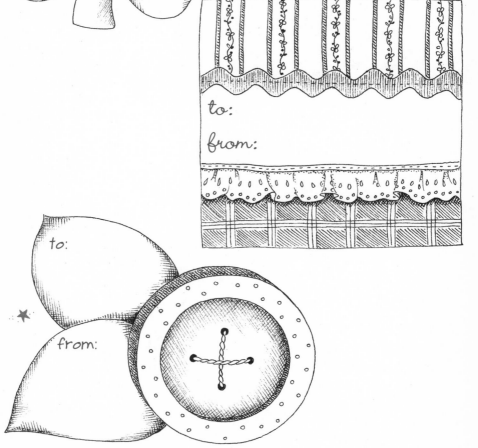

to:

from:

to:

from:

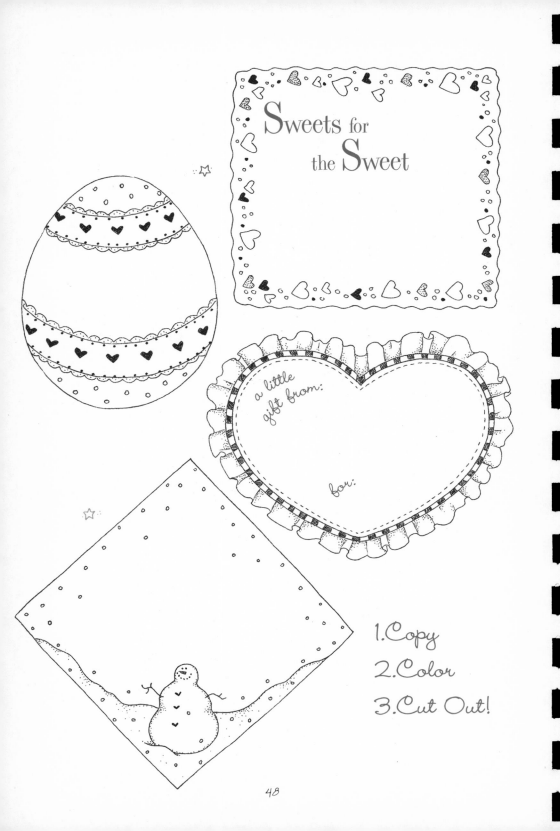

Sweets for
the Sweet

a little
gift from:

for:

1.Copy
2.Color
3.Cut Out!

48

April ★ May ★ June

"Gotcha!" Snack Mix

It's soooo good, it can't be healthy. April Fool!...it IS good for you!

6 qts. popped popcorn
2 12.3-oz. pkgs. bite-size
   whole-grain oat cereal
2 12-oz. cans mixed nuts
2 c. butter

2 c. brown sugar, packed
3/4 c. corn syrup
2-1/2 t. vanilla extract
1/2 t. baking soda

Combine first 3 ingredients together in a brown paper bag; shake to mix. Divide mixture equally between 2 large roasting pans; set aside. Add butter, brown sugar and corn syrup to a heavy saucepan; bring to a boil, stirring often. Boil 5 minutes; remove from heat. Stir in vanilla and baking soda; pour over popcorn mixtures, carefully tossing to coat. Bake at 250 degrees for one hour, stirring every 15 minutes; spread on sheets of aluminum foil to cool. Break into pieces; store in an airtight container. Makes about 7 quarts.

Fill a vintage metal picnic basket with "Gotcha!" Snack Mix, add a scoop and place paper bags nearby. Invite everyone to just help themselves to this nutty-sweet snack mix.

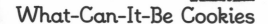

What-Can-It-Be Cookies

Have family and neighbors try to guess the main ingredient before they're allowed seconds...a tasty game for April 1st!

1 c. shortening	2 c. all-purpose flour
1-1/2 c. sugar, divided	1 t. baking soda
1 c. brown sugar, packed	1/2 t. baking powder
2 eggs	4 c. potato chips, crushed
1 t. vanilla extract	

Blend shortening, one cup sugar, brown sugar, eggs and vanilla together; add flour, baking soda and baking powder. Stir in crushed potato chips; mix well. Form into one-inch balls; roll in remaining sugar. Arrange 2 inches apart on ungreased baking sheets; flatten slightly with the bottom of cup dipped in sugar. Bake at 375 degrees for 8 to 10 minutes. Cool; drizzle with glaze. Makes about 4 dozen.

Glaze:

2-1/2 c. powdered sugar	3 T. milk
1/4 c. butter	1-1/2 t. vanilla extract
1/4 c. baking cocoa	

Place all ingredients except vanilla in a microwave-safe bowl; heat for 2 minutes. Stir in vanilla; heat and stir until smooth.

So easy...use colorful scrapbook papers to cover empty potato chip canisters, then fill each canister with cookies. Don't forget to add a bow and gift tag!

April ✴ May ✴ June

Delicious Dustpan Cookies

April 7th is No Housework Day...it's official, so put your feet up!

2 c. oil
2 c. sugar
2 c. brown sugar, packed
4 eggs
2 t. vanilla extract
4 c. all-purpose flour

1-1/2 t. salt
2 t. baking soda
1 c. flaked coconut
1-1/2 c. quick-cooking oats,
    uncooked
4 c. crispy rice cereal

Combine first 5 ingredients in a large mixing bowl; add remaining ingredients, one by one, mixing well after each addition. Cover dough with plastic wrap and chill for one to 2 hours. Drop dough by tablespoonfuls onto ungreased baking sheets; bake at 350 degrees until golden, about 10 to 14 minutes. Makes 5 to 6 dozen.

Whip up a batch of these cookies and deliver them all wrapped up on a sparkling new dustpan to your very best friend's house with a fun tag that says "Celebrate No Housework Day!"

Sweeter-than-Sugar Cake in a Jar

An oh-so-easy cake because it's mixed in the same pan it's baked!

2 c. all-purpose flour
2/3 c. baking cocoa
1 t. salt

1-1/2 t. baking powder
1-1/3 c. sugar

Layer ingredients in order listed in a one-quart, wide-mouth jar, packing firmly between layers; wipe sides of jar after adding baking cocoa. Secure lid; attach instructions.

Instructions:

Pour mix into an ungreased 13"x9" baking pan; stir in 3/4 cup oil, 2 teaspoons vinegar, one teaspoon vanilla extract and 2 cups water. Mix well. Bake at 350 degrees for 30 to 35 minutes; cool. Sprinkle with powdered sugar. Makes 18 servings.

Give Mom the day off along with a little TLC. Purchase-order forms can be found at any office supply store, fill one out with redeemable gifts. Ideas might include a manicure, an afternoon off and hugs, then make it the gift tag for this cake mix.

April ★ May ★ June

Bottom-Line Cornbread Baked in a Jar

We all know what day lands on April 15th...this is guaranteed to bring a lot of laughs!

1/3 c. cornmeal
2 T. all-purpose flour
1 T. sugar
1 t. pepper

1 t. onion salt
1-pint, wide-mouth canning jar
   and lid
8-oz. can creamed corn

Combine first 5 ingredients together; spoon into a plastic zipping bag. Seal; tuck into a one-pint, wide-mouth canning jar. Secure lid; tape creamed corn to the top. Attach instructions.

Instructions:

Place mix in a medium mixing bowl; mix in one egg, one tablespoon oil and creamed corn. Sterilize canning jar and lid; let cool. Spray with non-stick vegetable spray. Fill with cornbread mixture; place on an oven-proof glass pie plate. Bake at 350 degrees for 45 minutes. Cool slightly; scoop from jar to serve. Makes 4 to 6 servings.

Guaranteed giggles...set this mix inside a gift bag and instead of surrounding it with tissue paper, tuck in oodles of play money!

Penny-Pincher Potato Soup Mix

An easy-on-the-budget gift that will earn a million-dollar smile!

1-3/4 c. instant mashed potato
    flakes
1-1/2 c. powdered milk
2 T. chicken bouillon granules
2 t. dried, minced onion

2 t. dried parsley
1/4 t. white pepper
1/4 t. dried thyme
1/8 t. turmeric
1-1/2 t. seasoning salt

Combine all ingredients in a mixing bowl; spoon into a one-quart, wide-mouth jar. Secure lid. Attach instructions. Makes about 3-1/2 cups.

Instructions:

Place 1/2 cup mix in a bowl; add one cup boiling water. Stir until smooth. Makes one serving.

Decoupage play money to the outside of an empty cardboard oatmeal canister, then set a jar of Penny-Pincher Potato Soup Mix inside. Create a fun gift tag that looks like a giant penny!

April ★ May ★ June

Incredible Edible Easter Baskets

"No-bunny" can refuse these sweet treats!

18-oz. pkg. refrigerated sugar
    cookie dough
1 c. candy-coated chocolate
    mini-baking bits, divided
1 t. water

2 drops green food coloring
2/3 c. flaked coconut
3/4 c. vanilla frosting
red licorice whips, cut into
    36, 3-inch lengths

Divide dough into 36 pieces; roll into balls. Place in greased mini muffin cups; press dough over bottom and up the sides of each muffin cup. Refrigerate for 15 minutes. Sprinkle and press 1/3 cup mini-baking bits evenly into the bottoms and sides of dough cups; bake at 350 degrees until puffy, about 8 to 10 minutes. Remove from oven; gently press down dough with the back of a spoon. Return to oven for one additional minute; cool for 5 minutes. Remove to wire racks to cool completely. Combine water and food coloring in a medium mixing bowl; stir in coconut until tinted evenly. Layer one teaspoon frosting, one teaspoon coconut and one teaspoon remaining mini-baking bits into each muffin; bend licorice whips and insert into each cup for a basket handle, pushing into frosting. Store in an airtight container. Makes 3 dozen.

These little sweets are so darling...set inside
Easter grass-lined baskets to share with
friends & neighbors.

Carrot Cake Mix

Place in an Easter basket along with the can of pineapple and a large bunch of carrots...tie it all up in green cellophane.

2 c. sugar
3 c. all-purpose flour
1/4 t. nutmeg
1/4 t. cinnamon

2 t. vanilla powder
2 t. baking soda
1/2 c. chopped pecans
1 T. cinnamon

Combine ingredients in a medium mixing bowl; mix well. Spoon into an airtight container; attach instructions.

Instructions:

Place mix in a large mixing bowl; add 1-1/2 cups oil, 3 eggs, 3 cups grated carrots and an 8-ounce can crushed pineapple. Blend until smooth; spread in a greased 13"x9" baking pan. Bake at 350 degrees for 40 to 50 minutes or until a toothpick inserted in the center removes clean. Cool. Makes 15 servings.

For an "egg-cellent" idea, whitewash a market basket; let dry. Add whimsical stickers to the basket sides, then trim the rim with ribbon glued in place. Tuck the jar mix inside, along with some decorated eggs and a chocolate bunny.

April ✲ May ✲ June

Fanciful Easter Hat

So simple to make by just adding ribbons, trims and bits of jewelry…and your imagination!

hat
assorted ribbons
decorative buttons

vintage jewelry
needle & thread
hot glue gun & glue

Hand sew ribbon to the brim or crown of hat; add a bow. Center decorative button or vintage jewelry on bow, using hot glue. Embellish with remaining buttons and jewelry as desired securing with hot glue.

These hats are too pretty to tuck away after Easter!
Search local antique shops for
old-fashioned hat stands to display them on.

Mosaic Easter Eggs

Delight friends & family with Easter eggs decorated with bits of cut paper to create a mosaic effect!

printed magazine pictures or
   wrapping paper
1 doz. wooden eggs

small, flat paintbrush
decoupage medium

Tear magazine pictures or wrapping paper into small, irregularly shaped pieces. Dip paintbrush into decoupage medium and apply shapes to eggs in overlapping layers. When each egg is completely covered with the tiny cut-outs and has dried, apply a final coat of decoupage medium to seal the surface and add shine. Makes one dozen.

Fill a painted egg carton with paper grass to
nestle these beautiful eggs in, then tie up
with a colorful ribbon.

April ✴ May ✴ June

A Tisket, A Tasket, An Oatmeal-Filled Basket

*Blend together a basic oatmeal mix and then go crazy
with varieties sure to please everyone!*

3 c. quick-cooking oats,   1-1/2 t. salt, divided
   uncooked and divided   6 plastic zipping bags

Blend 1-1/2 cups oats at high speed until powdery; divide equally into each plastic bag. Put 1/4 cup remaining oats and 1/4 teaspoon salt into each bag; seal bags. Store in an airtight container. Attach instructions. Makes 6 bags.

Instructions:

Empty one bag into a bowl; add 3/4 cup boiling water. Stir and let stand for 2 minutes. Makes one serving.

Mix 'Em Up:

<u>Apples and Cinnamon</u>: To each bag, add one tablespoon sugar, 1/4 teaspoon cinnamon and 2 tablespoons chopped dried apples.

<u>Cinnamon Spice</u>: To each bag, add one tablespoon sugar, 1/4 teaspoon cinnamon and 1/8 teaspoon nutmeg.

<u>Raisins and Brown Sugar</u>: To each bag, add one tablespoon brown sugar and one tablespoon raisins.

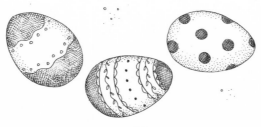

Sunflower Muffins

National Herb Week is the first week in May...share some warm muffins and herb plants from your garden with a friend.

2 c. biscuit baking mix
1/4 c. grated Parmesan cheese
1/4 c. plus 2 T. roasted
    sunflower kernels, divided
1/2 c. mayonnaise

1/4 c. milk
2 T. sugar
2-1/2 T. fresh chives, chopped
2 eggs

Combine all ingredients except for 2 tablespoons sunflower kernels; blend for 30 seconds. Set aside. Grease the bottoms only of muffin cups; fill 2/3 full with batter. Sprinkle each with remaining sunflower kernels; bake at 400 degrees until golden, 15 to 18 minutes. Makes one dozen.

A sure sign Summer is coming...give these muffins in a fabric-lined terra cotta pot. Don't forget to tuck in a bouquet of freshly picked herbs and daisies!

April ✦ May ✦ June

May Day Morning Coffee

Brew and deliver hot in a thermos to a friend's house to welcome May Day with a warm smile.

3-1/2 c. milk
1/3 c. instant coffee granules

1/4 c. brown sugar, packed
1 t. salt

Pour milk into a saucepan; heat until just boiling. Remove from heat; add remaining ingredients, stirring to dissolve. Makes 4 servings.

A coffee-loving friend will welcome a new spin on the traditional May Day bouquet. Use a beribboned handkerchief to hold a bag of fresh-roast coffee beans along with May Day Morning Coffee and coffee stir sticks. Tuck all these goodies inside a cone-shaped basket and slip over her doorknob.

Tea-rrific Coffee Squares

Tie up a plate of these in a bright tea towel...happy May Day!

1/2 c. oil	1 t. baking soda
2 c. brown sugar, packed	1 t. cinnamon
2 eggs	1 t. vanilla extract
3 c. all-purpose flour	1 c. brewed coffee
1 t. salt	2 c. chocolate chips
1 t. baking powder	

Combine oil, brown sugar and eggs in a large mixing bowl; mix well and set aside. Mix flour, salt, baking powder, baking soda and cinnamon together; add to sugar mixture. Blend in vanilla and coffee; fold in chocolate chips. Spread in a greased jelly-roll pan; bake at 350 degrees for 15 minutes. Cool and cut into squares to serve. Makes about 3 dozen.

Vintage tea towels can be found in such pretty
patterns and colors. For a welcome surprise, fill
a plate with Tea-rrific Coffee Squares, then wrap
the plate in a tea towel to match the colors in
a friend's kitchen.

April ★ May ★ June

THE Ring-Around-a-Rosie

So easy to fill with anyone's favorite toppings...a
Mother Goose Day (May 1st) special treat.

8-oz. tube refrigerated crescent
   rolls, separated
8 T. strawberry jam, divided

2 t. sugar, divided
1 drop red food coloring

Arrange rolls in a circle on a parchment paper-lined baking sheet with
wide ends slightly overlapping in the center and pointed ends facing
outward. Spoon one tablespoon jam in the center of each roll; sprinkle
dough evenly with one teaspoon sugar. Fold pointed ends of dough up
and over to the middle of the wide end, pinching to seal in place; set
aside. Place remaining sugar in a plastic zipping bag; add food
coloring, shaking to mix. Sprinkle over rolls; bake according to
package directions. Makes 8 servings.

to: from:

This jam-filled breakfast treat will be extra special if
given with a set of favorite Mother Goose books.
Wrap all the books together with
colorful lengths of rick-rack.

"Shhh!" Haystacks

Even Little Boy Blue will wake up for these easy snacks!

1-1/2 c. butterscotch chips
1/2 c. peanut butter

13-oz. pkg. chow mein noodles

Combine butterscotch chips and peanut butter in a double boiler; heat until melted, stirring occasionally. Remove from heat; mix in noodles until coated. Drop by teaspoonfuls onto a wax paper-lined baking sheet; refrigerate until firm. Makes about 2 dozen.

A pail filled with excelsior looks like hay, so why not
top it with lots of "Shhh!" Haystacks?
A whimsical surprise anyone will love!

April ★ May ★ June

Fajita Seasoning Mix

Cinco de Mayo (May 5th)...here's to liberty and freedom!

1 T. cornstarch	1/2 t. onion powder
2 t. chili powder	1/4 t. garlic powder
1 t. paprika	1/4 t. cayenne pepper
1 t. sugar	1/4 t. cumin
3/4 t. chicken bouillon granules	

Combine ingredients in a small, airtight container; secure lid. Attach instructions for Chicken Fajitas. Makes 1/4 cup.

Chicken Fajitas:

4 boneless, skinless chicken breasts, sliced into thin strips	1/3 c. water
	1 green pepper, sliced
	1 onion, sliced
2 T. oil	6 8-inch tortillas

Sauté chicken in hot oil in a 10" skillet for 5 minutes; add all of the Fajita Seasoning Mix. Add remaining ingredients except for tortillas; sauté until juices run clear when chicken is pierced with a fork, about 5 additional minutes. Place tortillas on a microwave-safe plate; cover with plastic wrap and microwave on high for one minute. Spoon chicken mixture down the center of each tortilla; roll up jelly-roll style. Serve warm. Makes 6.

El Taco Paloma

*The Mexican name for popcorn is paloma which means dove...kernels
of popcorn are palomitas or little doves!*

2 qts. popped popcorn	1 T. taco seasoning mix
1 c. tortilla chips, crushed	1/2 c. grated Cheddar cheese
3 T. butter	

Combine popcorn and tortilla chips in a large bowl; set aside. Melt
butter over low heat; stir in taco seasoning mix. Remove from heat;
drizzle over popcorn. Toss to coat thoroughly; spread in a greased
jelly-roll pan. Sprinkle with cheese; place under broiler for one minute,
watching constantly. Remove and cool before serving. Makes about
12 servings.

The best way to give popcorn is in a giant popcorn tin
along with movie rental coupons and bottles
of frosty soda pop!

April ✶ May ✶ June

Oh-So-Simple Piñata

This quick & easy version of a piñata makes it a terrific activity to do with the kids...and it's a lot less messy than the paper maché version!

paper grocery or lunch bag
newspaper
candy or other treats
crêpe paper in favorite colors

scissors
craft glue
hole punch
string

Fill paper bag with candy and treats; scrunch up a piece of newspaper and tuck inside the bag until completely full. Set aside. Cut strips of crêpe paper long enough to wrap around the bag; fringe by cutting about 1/2 way up along the length, one to 4 inches apart. Starting at the bottom of the bag, glue on strips; overlap strips slightly until entire bag is covered. Remember to glue only the uncut part, without getting any glue on the fringes. Punch holes around the top of the bag; lace a length of string through the holes, pulling tight. Tie on a loop for hanging. Cut 4 or 5 long strips of crêpe paper and glue them to the bottom of the bag for streamers.

For festive fun on Cinco de Mayo, decorate indoors or out with lots of brightly colored lanterns...so easy.

Colorful Painted Stemware

Create an instant fiesta atmosphere! Set the table with these beautiful painted glasses.

newspaper
drinking glasses
star-shaped stickers
wooden craft stick
etching cream

red, gold or silver paint pens
2 pkgs. red craft jewels
super-strength glue

Spread newspaper over work surface. Wash and dry glasses thoroughly; arrange on newspaper. Apply stickers to prevent etching cream from reaching glass and to create a star design. Use craft stick to apply etching cream to glass; let dry 10 minutes then rinse with warm water. Remove stickers and outline star shapes with paint pens. Using a dab of glue, apply jewels inside each star. Glasses should be washed by hand.

Why not share some painted glasses with a friend? Wrap each glass in colorful bubble wrap, then set inside a painted tin. Painting the tin is easy...just stencil red hot peppers on a white tin, then tie on strands of raffia to secure the tag.

April ★ May ★ June

Lemony Chicken Salad

A refreshing and delicious luncheon dish for Mothers' Day.
And if you'd like, it's easy to spoon this salad into hollowed-out
cherry tomatoes for bite-size appetizers.

3/4 c. cooked chicken, chopped
2 T. celery, finely chopped
1 T. scallions, finely chopped
3 T. mayonnaise-type salad
    dressing
1/4 t. lemon zest

1 t. lemon juice
5 to 6 tomatoes, halved
1/2 c. fresh spinach, finely
    chopped
2 t. chopped almonds, toasted

Blend together chicken, celery and scallions. Stir in salad dressing,
lemon zest and lemon juice. Refrigerate, covered, for at least
30 minutes to chill thoroughly. Scoop out and discard tomato pulp,
leaving 1/4-inch shells. Place tomato shells, cut-side down, on
paper towels for 30 minutes. Blend spinach, almonds and chicken
mixture; spoon into each tomato shell. Serve immediately. Makes
10 to 12 servings.

When giving Mom
something special this
Mothers' Day, why not
make the package special
too? Jewelry, soothing
sachets or fragrant soaps
can all be nicely tucked
inside a simple white box
filled with fresh rose petals
and tied up
with a silk ribbon.

to: The Greatest Mom!

Warm & Fuzzy Mothers' Day Slippers

Mom will love slipping into these cozy and oh-so-easy to make slippers for her special day.

1 pr. white fleece slippers
2 4-inch sqs. colorful felted
   wool

4-inch sq. fusible web
embroidery thread & needle
2 buttons

Following manufacturer's instructions, fuse felt squares together with layer of fusible web. Cut two flower shapes from fused layers and blanket-stitch edges using embroidery thread. Stitch button through center of flower and onto center of slipper.

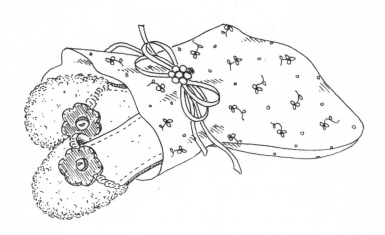

Place Mom's new slippers inside a pretty fabric pouch topped off with a vintage clip-on earring and length of velvet ribbon.

April ★ May ★ June

No-Need-to-Bake Cheesecake

Sprinkle with blueberries for a true red, white & blue Flag Day (June 14th) pie.

8-oz. pkg. cream cheese, softened
14-oz. can sweetened condensed milk

1/3 c. lemon juice
1 t. vanilla extract
9-inch graham cracker pie crust
21-oz. can cherry pie filling

Blend cream cheese until light and fluffy; add milk, mixing well. Mix in lemon juice and vanilla; blend until smooth. Spread into pie crust; refrigerate until firm, about 3 hours. Spread with pie filling. Makes 8 servings.

When toting yummy No-Need-to-Bake Cheesecake to a Flag Day picnic, bring along some patriotic painted terra cotta pots to hold silverware and napkins. It's easy...just add alternating red and white stripes to the bottom of the pot and paint the rim blue. When dry, top off the blue rim with white stars. When all the paint has thoroughly dried, protect it with acrylic sealer.

Go-Fly-a-Kite Cupcakes

Go-Fly-a-Kite Day is usually celebrated on the same day as Flag Day ...June 14.

1-2/3 c. all-purpose flour
1/2 c. baking cocoa
1 t. baking powder
1/2 t. baking soda
1/4 t. salt
1-3/4 c. sugar
1/4 c. brown sugar, packed

1/2 c. shortening
1 c. buttermilk
3 eggs
2 T. oil
3/4 t. vanilla extract
1/2 c. candy-coated chocolate
  mini-baking bits

Combine first 5 ingredients; add sugars, tossing to mix. Blend in shortening; add remaining ingredients except candy-coated chocolates, mixing well. Fill paper-lined muffin cups 2/3 full; sprinkle each with one teaspoon candy-coated chocolates. Bake at 350 degrees for 20 to 25 minutes; cool completely on wire racks. Decorate with a graham kite. Makes 2 dozen.

Graham Cracker Kites:

24 graham cracker squares
16-oz. container white frosting,
  divided

assorted food colorings
1 c. candy-coated chocolate
  mini-baking bits

Using a serrated knife, gently cut graham cracker squares into kite shapes; set aside. Tint half the frosting to desired kite color; tint remaining frosting sky blue. Frost cupcakes with sky blue frosting; frost graham kites with remaining frosting. Arrange mini-baking bits from corner to corner on graham kites; tilt cracker slightly and stick onto cupcake top. Add a string tail of mini-baking bits.

April ★ May ★ June

Cheddar Spread

June is National Dairy Month and this tasty spread will get everyone in the "moo-o-o-d" to celebrate!

1 c. mayonnaise
1 t. Worcestershire sauce
1/2 t. garlic salt

4 c. shredded sharp Cheddar
   cheese
4-oz. jar pimentos, drained

Combine first 3 ingredients together until smooth; mix in cheese and pimentos. Cover in an airtight container and keep refrigerated. Makes about 4-1/2 cups.

Share some smiles! Slip a jar of Cheddar Spread and some crispy crackers inside a white lunch bag that's been sponge painted with black acrylic paint and tied closed with a red gingham bow.

Cheesy Herb Muffins in a Jar

A zesty side that's just right with grilled pork chops or chicken.

2-1/2 c. all-purpose flour
1/4 c. cornmeal
1/4 c. sugar
1 T. baking powder
1 t. baking soda
1 t. salt

1/4 t. cayenne pepper
1/2 c. grated Parmesan cheese
1/3 c. powdered buttermilk
1 T. dried chives
1-1/2 t. red pepper flakes

Layer all ingredients in the order listed in a one-quart, wide-mouth jar; secure lid. Attach instructions.

Instructions:

Place mix in a large mixing bowl; stir in 2 eggs, 1-1/2 cups water and 1/4 cup oil until just moistened. Fill greased muffin cups 2/3 full with batter; bake at 400 degrees until golden, about 20 minutes. Makes one dozen.

A friend who enjoys gardening will love a crate filled with surprises! Add Cheesy Herb Muffins in a Jar, a pair of garden gloves, trowel and seed packets.

April ★ May ★ June

Hamburger Seasoning Mix

June 21st officially welcomes Summer and it's time to fire up the grill!

1-1/4 t. pepper
3 T. onion powder
1 T. garlic powder
1 t. salt

1-2/3 c. powdered milk
1/3 c. dried, minced onion
3-1/2 T. beef bouillon granules
2 T. dried parsley

Combine ingredients; store in an airtight container. Attach instructions. Makes about 2-1/2 cups.

Burgers:

Add one or 2 tablespoons Hamburger Seasoning Mix to one pound ground beef before forming into patties to grill. Makes 4.

Cheeseburger Casserole:

Brown one pound ground beef in a 12" skillet; add one cup uncooked elbow macaroni, 1/2 cup Hamburger Seasoning Mix, 2 cups water and 10-3/4 ounce can tomato soup. Bring mixture to a boil; stir, reduce heat and simmer for 20 minutes. Remove from heat; stir in 1/2 cup shredded Cheddar cheese. Serve warm. Serves 4.

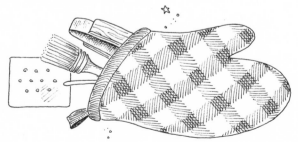

To celebrate Fathers' Day, the 3rd Sunday in June, what Dad wouldn't love use a new set of tongs, oven mitts, basting brush and his very own chef's apron?

Chili Burger Mix

Spice up your burgers...have plenty of lemonade and iced tea on hand!

1 T. all-purpose flour
1-1/2 t. chili powder
1/2 t. red pepper flakes
1/2 t. sugar

2 T. dried, minced onion
1 t. seasoned salt
1/2 t. dried, minced garlic
1/2 t. cumin

Combine all ingredients; store in an airtight container in a cool, dry cupboard for up to 6 months. Attach instructions. Makes about 1/4 cup.

Instructions:

Combine one to 1-1/2 tablespoons mix with one pound ground beef; mix well. Form into patties; grill to desired doneness. Makes 4.

Pack both the Chili Burger and Hamburger Seasoning Mixes into a barbecue gift bag for a much-appreciated host or hostess surprise! Cut 2 back pockets from a pair of old blue jeans, arrange on the front of a white gift bag and secure with hot glue. Slip a sassy red bandanna in one pocket and a gift card in the other.

April ✴ May ✴ June

Best-Dad-in-the-Land BBQ Rub

Rub about 1/3 cup mix into beef brisket at least 2 hours before cooking...an easy mix to add to a Fathers' Day grilling gift.

16-oz. bottle seasoned salt
1/4 c. paprika
2/3 c. chili powder
1 t. ground ginger
1 t. nutmeg
2 t. dry mustard

1 t. ground cloves
1 t. mesquite-flavored seasoning mix
2 T. garlic salt
1-1/2 T. pepper
1 c. brown sugar, packed

Combine all ingredients in a mixing bowl; mix well. Store in an airtight container in a dry, cool place for up to 6 weeks. Makes about 3 cups.

Pick up a photo tube at any camera shop to slip this spicy BBQ rub into. Make a black & white photocopy of one of Dad's favorite photos, scale it to fit the tube and secure with spray adhesive. He'll love it!

Dad's Favorite Steak Sauce

No need for that catsup bottle when this sauce is in town!

3 T. raspberry jam
2 T. brown sugar, packed
2 T. Worcestershire sauce
2 T. tomato sauce

2 T. malt vinegar
5 drops hot pepper sauce
salt and pepper to taste

Whisk ingredients together in a medium saucepan; bring to a boil over high heat. Reduce heat and simmer until thickened, about 10 minutes; stir frequently. Makes 1/2 cup.

This Fathers' Day tell Dad to "Go Fishing!" Fill a fishing creel basket with goodies for his big barbecue...Dad's Favorite Steak Sauce, Best-Dad-in-the-Land BBQ Rub and grilling tools. Afterward, he can fill the fishing creel with everything he'll need for a lazy day in the sun trying to catch "the big one!"

April ★ May ★ June

Baked Sesame Sticks

An easy take-along snack for munching during ball games.

2 c. buttermilk biscuit baking
    mix
2/3 c. milk

1/3 c. butter, melted
2 t. sesame seed, toasted

Combine baking mix and milk; blend on medium-low speed of an electric mixer for 10 seconds. Knead on a lightly floured surface until smooth, about 10 to 12 times; roll out into a 10"x6" rectangle. Slice into 2"x1/2" strips; arrange in an ungreased jelly-roll pan. Spread with melted butter, turning to coat both sides; sprinkle with sesame seed. Cover with plastic wrap; refrigerate for one to 2 hours. Bake at 450 degrees until golden, about 12 to 18 minutes; cool to room temperature. Store in an airtight container. Makes one dozen.

Coat tin pails with green acrylic paint; let dry.
Paint on baseballs with white acrylic paint, and then
use red dimensional paint for the
baseball stitching. Filled with Baked Sesame Sticks,
it's a terrific way to tote snacks
to any home team game!

Hickory-Smoked Popcorn Mix

National Little League Baseball Week begins the second Monday in June and the whole team will cheer when it comes to this tasty treat!

4 qts. popped popcorn	1/2 t. seasoned salt
2 c. mini pretzels	1 t. hickory-smoked salt
1 c. peanuts	1/2 c. grated Parmesan cheese
1/3 c. butter, melted	1/2 c. bacon bits

Place popcorn, pretzels and peanuts in a large mixing bowl; toss gently and set aside. Whisk butter and salts together; pour over popcorn mixture, stirring to coat. Sprinkle with cheese and bacon bits; serve warm. Serves 12.

For a sure hit, serve up Hickory-Smoked Popcorn Mix in baseball sacks! Fill a green gift sack with snack mix; fold the top of the bag over and glue to close. Use a white paint pen to write "Let's Play Ball!" across the fold; let dry. Paint a round wooden cut-out with white acrylic paint and when dry, add stitching to the cut-out using a red permanent felt-tip pen; hot glue to the center of the bag.

April ⋆ May ⋆ June

"Congratulations!" Caramel Squares

Wrap up individually and place in a graduation cap...don't forget to add a diploma declaring "Great job, graduate!"

1-1/2 c. brown sugar, packed
   and divided
1/2 c. margarine, softened
2 eggs, separated

1 t. vanilla extract
1-1/2 c. all-purpose flour
2 t. baking powder
1/4 c. chopped nuts

Combine 1/2 cup brown sugar, margarine, egg yolks, vanilla, flour and baking powder; mix well. Press into a greased 8"x8" baking pan; set aside. Whisk egg whites until stiff; gradually blend in remaining brown sugar. Spread over crust; sprinkle with nuts. Bake at 325 degrees until golden, about 25 minutes. Cool; cut into squares. Makes 1-1/2 dozen.

Every new college student will appreciate a "Survival Kit" filled with all the necessities of college life. Fill a small vintage suitcase with "Congratulations!" Caramel Squares, instant soup and cocoa mixes, a phone card, day planner, pens, pencils, highlighters and gift certificates for school supplies, groceries and books.

Butter-Toffee Popcorn with Almonds

Kindergarten graduates to Ph. D's will appreciate a tin full of this golden snack.

4 qts. popped popcorn
1/2 c. toasted almonds
3/4 c. sugar
1/4 c. brown sugar, packed
1/2 c. butter

1/2 c. corn syrup
1/2 c. water
1/2 t. salt
1/2 t. vanilla extract

Toss popcorn and almonds together; spread evenly in 2 buttered jelly-roll pans. Place in oven at lowest temperature. Combine the remaining ingredients except for vanilla in a large saucepan over medium heat; stir and heat until mixture reaches 265 to 275 degrees on a candy thermometer. Remove from heat; stir in vanilla. Pour over popcorn mixture, stirring to coat completely. Spread mixture on wax paper; cool. Break into pieces; store in an airtight container. Makes about 4 quarts.

If high school grads are traveling away to college, help prepare them for the trip. For nibbling, spoon this buttery snack mix into a box wrapped with a map. Give along with a cooler of fresh fruit, bottles of juice and water, cheese & crackers and a sandwich or 2 for the drive.

April ★ May ★ June

Frosty Candy Bar Cookies in a Jar

Attach a sleeve of favorite candy bars...with instructions to freeze, of course!

2 c. all-purpose flour   1/2 c. brown sugar, packed
1 t. baking soda   1/2 c. sugar
1-1/2 t. vanilla powder

Layer ingredients in the order listed in a one-quart, wide-mouth jar; secure lid. Attach instructions.

Instructions:

Cream one cup softened butter until fluffy in a large mixing bowl; add one egg, blending well. Mix in cookie mix and one cup coarsely broken frozen candy bars; blend until just moistened. Shape dough into 1-1/2 inch balls; arrange 2 inches apart on ungreased baking sheets. Bake at 350 degrees for 10 to 12 minutes; cool on baking sheets for 2 minutes. Remove to wire rack to cool completely. Makes about 3 dozen.

School's out and the kids need a snack, what's a busy mom to do? Help her out by giving this easy-to-make cookie mix along with a whimsical photo frame for school pictures. To make the frame, just decoupage or use craft glue to attach pencils and wooden letters around the frame...it's a snap!

Bucket of Cookie Mix

Mix up a batch right when school lets out...makes baking cookies a breeze even in the summertime heat.

5 c. all-purpose flour
3-3/4 c. sugar
2 T. baking powder

2 t. salt
1-1/2 c. plus 2 T. butter,
    softened

Combine first 4 ingredients in a very large mixing bowl; mix well. Cut in butter with a pastry blender until coarse crumbs form; place in an airtight container. Keep in the refrigerator for up to 3 months. Makes 10 cups.

Sunshine Cookies:

Bring 4 cups mix to room temperature in a mixing bowl; add one egg, one tablespoon lemon zest and 1-1/2 tablespoons lemon juice, mixing well. Divide dough in half; form each into a 1-1/2 inch in diameter roll. Wrap dough in plastic wrap; refrigerate until firm, about 2 hours. Slice dough into 1/8-inch slices; arrange one inch apart on greased baking sheets. Sprinkle with sugar; bake at 350 degrees for 8 minutes. Remove to a wire rack to cool completely. Makes about 4 dozen.

Brownies:

Melt one cup semi-sweet chocolate chips; let cool 5 minutes. Place in a mixing bowl; mix in 2 cups room-temperature mix, 2 eggs and one teaspoon vanilla extract. Spread in a greased 8"x8" baking pan; bake at 350 degrees for 20 minutes. Set aside to cool. Melt one cup peanut butter chips; drizzle over the top. Cool. Cut into squares to serve. Makes 16.

April ✳ May ✳ June

Amish Friendship Bread

Share your starter with a friend.

3 c. flour, divided
3 c. sugar, divided
3 c. milk, divided
2/3 c. oil
2 c. flour
1 c. sugar
1-1/4 t. baking powder

3 eggs
1-1/2 to 2 t. cinnamon
1 t. vanilla
1/2 t. salt
1/2 t. baking soda

Make your own starter by combining one cup flour, one cup sugar and one cup of milk in a non-metal bowl. On day one, the day you make or receive your starter, do nothing. On days 2, 3 and 4, stir with a wooden spoon. Do not use a metal spoon. Day 5 add one cup flour, one cup sugar and one cup milk; stir. Days 6, 7, 8 and 9, stir with wooden spoon. Day 10 add one cup flour, one cup sugar and one cup milk; stir. To give the starter as gifts, pour one cup of the starter into 3 glass or plastic containers and give to 2 friends, keeping one starter for yourself. To the remaining batch, add the remainder of the ingredients. Pour into 2 well-greased and sugared loaf pans. Bake at 350 degrees for 40 to 50 minutes. Cool 10 minutes before removing from pan. Be sure to include these instructions on your gift tag when giving your starter away!

A muslin bag stenciled with a bright red apple is the perfect way to give a jar of Carnival Apple Jelly. Tie closed with a length of jute and gift tag that reads "1st Place Friend!"

Funnel Cake Mix

Golden swirls of fair-time goodness.

1-2/3 c. all-purpose flour   1/2 t. cream of tartar
1/2 t. salt   2 T. sugar
3/4 t. baking soda

Combine all ingredients; place in a plastic zipping bag. Seal; attach instructions.

Instructions:

Whisk one egg and one cup milk together in a large mixing bowl; blend in mix and set aside. Heat one inch oil in a deep frying pan to 375 degrees; pour half cupfuls batter through a funnel into oil with a circular motion forming a spiral. Heat until golden; flip and heat until golden on both sides. Remove and drain on paper towels; sprinkle with powdered sugar. Makes 6 to 8.

Give Funnel Cake Mix in a shiny tin can. Just use craft glue to attach black button eyes to a silver coffee can; add fabric circles for cheeks and a triangle nose. A black pipe cleaner easily glues on to become a mouth. Then, place mix inside can, secure lid and glue the funnel on lid for the hat!

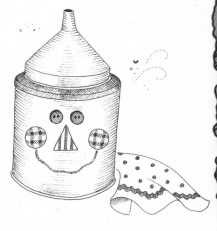

April ✶ May ✶ June

Candy Strawberries

June is National Candy Month...indulge your sweet tooth!

2 3-oz. pkgs. strawberry gelatin
   mix
1 c. flaked coconut
1 c. chopped pecans

3/4 c. sweetened condensed
   milk
1 t. vanilla extract
red sanding sugar

Combine first 3 ingredients; mix well. Blend in milk and vanilla; cover and refrigerate for one hour. Shape into strawberries; roll in sanding sugar. Arrange on a serving plate; chill until serving. Makes 2 dozen.

Since these Candy Strawberries need to be served chilled, fill a plastic zipping bag with crushed ice and set inside a strawberry basket. Use a paper shredder and colored paper to make pretty filling to cover the bag, then arrange candies on top. Be sure to deliver right away!

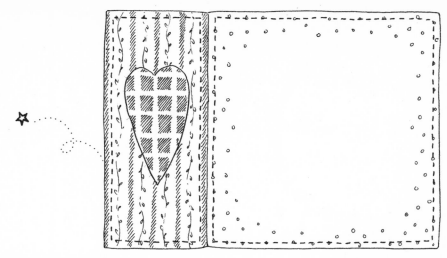

to:

from:

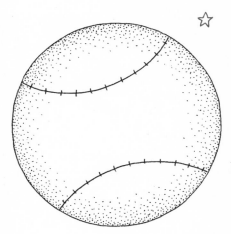

Have some fun with these
tags; copy, color
and share!

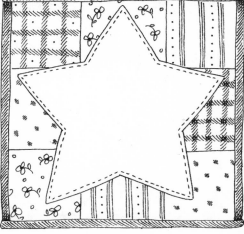

To:

Just copy and go!

from the kitchen of:

July
August
September

July ★ August ★ September

Old Glory Cookies in a Jar

Use tie-dyed candy-coated chocolates for beach day, orange and yellow ones for Halloween, red and green for Christmas...a versatile mix great for any celebration!

1-1/4 c. sugar
1-1/4 c. red, white & blue
   candy-coated chocolates

2 c. all-purpose flour
1/2 t. baking soda
1/2 t. baking powder

Layer sugar and then chocolates in a one-quart, wide-mouth jar; press each layer firmly. Set aside. Combine remaining ingredients; pack firmly on top of chocolate layer. Secure lid; attach instructions.

Instructions:

Place mix in a large mixing bowl; add 1/2 cup softened butter, one beaten egg and 1-1/2 teaspoons vanilla extract. Mix well. Shape dough into one-inch balls; arrange 2 inches apart on greased baking sheets. Bake at 375 degrees for 12 to 15 minutes; cool on wire racks. Makes about 2-1/2 dozen.

Give this jar in a star-spangled gift bag! Follow manufacturer's instructions to place paper-backed fusible web onto fabric. Cut fabric the same size as a lunch bag; remove paper backing and fuse fabric to bag. Fold top edge of bag down to make a cuff and use hot glue to attach a small flag...so simple!

Ka-Boom Snack Mix

*Wow the crowd at the next Independence Day celebration
with this crispy-crunchy treat!*

6 c. popped popcorn
4 c. bite-size crispy rice cereal
   squares

7-oz. jar marshmallow creme
1/4 c. red, white & blue jimmies

Combine popcorn and cereal in a large bowl; set aside. Microwave
marshmallow creme, uncovered, on high for one minute; stir.
Microwave and stir in 30-second intervals until melted. Pour over
popcorn mixture; stir until coated. Sprinkle with jimmies; spread on
a lightly buttered baking sheet. Bake at 350 degrees for 5 minutes;
stir. Bake until golden, about 5 additional minutes. Spread on wax
paper to cool; break apart and store in an airtight container for up to
2 weeks. Makes about 10 cups.

Decorate a clean, empty coffee
can with stars & stripes using
acrylic paint. Punch a hole in
the lid and slip a licorice
"fuse" through. Filled with
Ka-Boom Snack Mix, this
makes a poppin' good
fireworks snack!

July ★ August ★ September

Star-Shaped Bubble Wand

An easy make-ahead that will entertain the kids while they're waiting for the fireworks to begin.

40-inch length of 20-gauge wire   electric drill
star-shaped cookie cutter   enamel spray paint
wire cutters

Fold wire in half, then beginning at one point of the star cookie cutter, bend the wire around the cutter to form the star shape. When the wire is completely covering the cookie cutter, twist to secure. Straighten the ends of the remaining wire and cut with wire cutters to make both ends even in length. Place the trimmed ends into the chuck on an electric drill and tighten the chuck. Hold the wire tightly and rotate the drill until the wire is completely twisted and tight. Coat bubble wand with spray paint; let dry.

Fill a painted pail with bubble wands and flags held in place with bright marbles. A colorful picnic center-piece until they're ready to be put to use!

Starry Picnic Basket

So festive, this basket can be made in a jiffy!

bushel basket
white gel stain
3 foam paintbrushes

red & blue acrylic paints
wooden star cut-outs
hot glue gun & glue

Coat basket with white gel stain using a foam brush; let dry. Repeat if desired. Paint wooden stars, alternating paint colors of red and blue. When stars are dry, use hot glue to attach stars to basket rim.

Watching fireworks at a friend's house? Fill this star-studded basket with cheese, crackers, snack mixes and frosty bottles of root beer...an ideal hostess gift!

Marshmallow Ice Cream Topping

*National Hot Fudge Sundae Day is July 25...whip up a topping bar,
gather waffle cones and sugar cones and invite
some friends over to share a cool dessert!*

3/4 c. sugar
1 T. corn syrup
1/4 c. milk
2-1/2 T. butter

8-oz. pkg. marshmallows
2 T. water
1-1/2 t. vanilla extract

Add first 4 ingredients to a large, heavy saucepan; heat over
low heat until sugar dissolves, stirring often. Increase heat and bring
to a boil; reduce heat and simmer 5 minutes. Melt marshmallows
in a double boiler with water; remove from heat. Stir in vanilla and
hot sugar mixture; mix well. Store in an airtight container in the
refrigerator until use; reheat and serve warm. Makes about 2 cups.

Cherry Ice Cream Topping

Looks as good as it tastes!

2 c. canned cherries, drained
    with juice reserved
1/3 c. sugar
1/4 c. corn syrup

1 T. lemon juice
2 t. cornstarch
1 T. water

Heat cherry juice in a heavy saucepan over medium heat; add
sugar, corn syrup and lemon juice. Whisk cornstarch and water
together; gradually stir into cherry juice mixture. Heat and stir until
thick; remove from heat. Stir in cherries; serve warm. Makes about
2-1/2 cups.

Summertime Snowballs

These deep-fried ice cream balls will melt in your mouth!

4 scoops ice cream, rounded
1 egg, beaten
1/2 t. vanilla extract
2-1/2 c. corn flake cereal,
    crushed

1/2 t. cinnamon
oil for deep frying

Arrange ice cream balls in a freezer-proof 8"x8" pan; freeze until firm, at least one hour. Whisk egg and vanilla together in a small bowl; set aside. Toss cereal and cinnamon together; spread in a shallow pie plate. Dip each ice cream ball into egg mixture; roll in cereal mixture until well coated. Freeze until firm, at least one hour. Deep fry ice cream balls, one at a time, in 375-degree oil until golden, about 15 seconds; drain on paper towels. Return fried ice cream balls to freezer until all are fried; serve at once. Makes 4 servings.

Celebrate Summer! These Summertime Snowballs are
a delightful surprise when tucked inside
a child's sand bucket!

July ★ August ★ September

Orange Float Mix

A yummy warm-weather treat that can be shared year 'round.

4 c. powdered milk
2 c. unsweetened orange drink
   mix

1 c. sugar
1 c. powdered whole egg

Combine all ingredients in a large mixing bowl; mix well. Place in an airtight container; store in a cool, dry place and use within 6 months. Attach instructions. Makes 8 cups.

Instructions:

Place 1/2 cup mix and one cup water into a blender; add 2 to 3 ice cubes. Blend well; serve immediately. Makes one serving.

Fill a large glass jar with this drink mix, add a pair of sporty sunglasses and a visor for a gift that's made in the shade!

Chocolate Malt Cookies in a Jar

Brings back memories of the soda counter in the 5 & dime store!

2-1/2 c. all-purpose flour
3/4 c. malted milk powder
1/2 t. baking soda
1/2 t. salt

1/2 c. brown sugar, packed
1 c. sugar
2 c. semi-sweet chocolate chips

Combine first 4 ingredients together; pack firmly into a one-quart, wide-mouth jar. Add brown sugar, sugar and then chocolate chips; pack each ingredient firmly before adding the next, placing any chocolate chips that may not fit in a plastic zipping bag. Secure lid; attach instructions and plastic zipping bag, if necessary.

Instructions:

Cream one cup softened butter in a large mixing bowl; add 2 eggs, one teaspoon vanilla extract and 2 tablespoons sweetened condensed milk. Mix well. Add mix; blend until combined. Drop 2 inches apart by rounded tablespoonfuls onto ungreased baking sheets; bake at 300 degrees until golden, 24 to 28 minutes. Transfer to a wire rack to cool completely. Makes about 3-1/2 dozen.

Take a friend back to the "good old days" with this malted cookie mix. Fill a basket with mix, a school pennant, pom-poms, bottles of soda and a picture of the two of you in high school!

July ⋆ August ⋆ September

3-Pepper Relish

The perfect garden offering for any cookout host and a canning recipe that's a snap to make.

2 red peppers, minced
2 green peppers, minced
10 jalapeño peppers, seeded and
   minced
1 c. cider vinegar

5-1/4 c. sugar
1 t. butter
1 pouch powdered fruit pectin
6 1/2-pint canning jars and
   lids, sterilized

Measure one cup each of red peppers, green peppers and jalapeño peppers and place in a heavy 6-quart saucepan; refrigerate any remaining peppers for use in another recipe. Stir in vinegar, sugar and butter; bring mixture to a rolling boil over high heat, stirring constantly. Add pectin; return to rolling boil, stirring constantly. Boil for one minute; remove from heat. Skim off any foam using a metal spoon; ladle into jars, leaving 1/8-inch headspace. Wipe rims; secure lids and rings. Invert jars for 5 minutes; turn upright or process in a boiling water bath for 15 minutes. Set aside to cool 24 hours. Check for seals; use within 6 months. Makes 6 jars.

Search out vintage fabrics in splashy vegetable prints, then make color photocopies. Cut out squares and attach to the front of a small brown paper bag using spray adhesive. Set jar of relish inside, turn down bag edges and tie on a gift tag...so easy!

just for you!

Homemade Mustard

It's so easy to make and what a pleasant homemade gift to receive!

2-1/3 c. sugar
1-1/3 c. dry mustard
6 eggs, beaten

1-1/3 c. white vinegar
5 1/2-pint canning jars and
   lids, sterilized

Combine sugar and mustard in a large saucepan; heat over low heat, gradually stirring in eggs and vinegar. Whisk over low heat until thickened. Ladle into canning jars, leaving 1/8-inch headspace; secure lids and rings. Process in a boiling water bath for 15 minutes; remove from heat. Set jars aside; check for seals after 12 hours. Refrigerate after opening. Makes 5 jars.

Quick Hot & Sweet Mustard

Wonderful when spread over just-grilled pork chops.

1/3 c. brown mustard seed
3 T. cider vinegar
1 T. olive oil

1/2 t. honey
1/8 t. dried tarragon

Grind mustard seeds in a spice grinder; place in a small mixing bowl. Add remaining ingredients; stir until smooth and thick. Refrigerate in an airtight container until serving. Makes 1/2 cup.

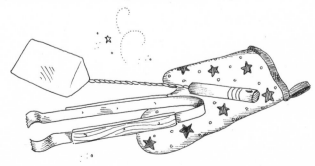

July ★ August ★ September

Boston Baked Beans Mix

*July is National Picnic Month...so enjoy some yummy baked beans
with a juicy burger, side of potato salad and
a tall icy glass of lemonade.*

2 c. dried white pea beans	1/2 t. pepper
1/2 t. dried thyme	2 t. salt
1 bay leaf	2 T. dry mustard
1/4 t. ground ginger	

Place ingredients in a large plastic zipping bag; shake to combine.
Attach instructions.

Instructions:

Place 2 slices chopped bacon, 4-3/4 cups water, 3/4 cup chopped
onion, one minced clove garlic, 3 tablespoons molasses and bean
mix into a slow cooker; stir to combine. Heat on low setting for 10 to
12 hours; stir occasionally. Remove bay leaf before serving. Serves 8.

Beat the summer heat...share
this Boston Baked Beans Mix in
a cool watermelon pail!
Sponge pink acrylic paint
inside a metal pail; let dry.
Paint the outside of the pail
light green, then sponge on
darker green stripes. When the
pail has thoroughly dried,
apply acrylic spray sealer both
inside and outside.

Parmesan Herb Salad Dressing Mix

Tuck into a basket with a bottle of olive oil and a small jar filled with cider vinegar...don't forget the instructions!

3 T. grated Parmesan cheese
1 T. dried parsley
1 t. dried, minced onion
1 t. sugar
1/4 t. dried oregano

1/4 t. dried basil
1/4 t. dried thyme
1/4 t. garlic powder
1/2 t. pepper

Spoon all ingredients into a small plastic zipping bag; seal. Attach instructions.

Instructions:

Pour 1/2 cup olive oil into a one-pint jar; add 1/4 cup cider vinegar and seasoning mix. Secure lid; shake to combine. Makes 3/4 cup.

For a gift basket in a flash, use a black paint pen to add a row of marching ants across the wooden handle of a basket! Lined with a red-checked napkin, add a bag of dressing mix and tie on a simple shipping tag label...it's a sure winner!

July ✦ August ✦ September

Brownies Baked in a Jar

Wide-mouth jars are a must or the brownies can't slide out!

1 c. all-purpose flour
1 c. sugar
1/2 t. baking soda
1/4 t. cinnamon
1/3 c. margarine, softened
1/4 c. water
3 T. baking cocoa

1/4 c. buttermilk, room
   temperature
1 egg, beaten
1/2 t. vanilla extract
3 1-pint, wide-mouth canning
   jars and lids, sterilized

Combine first 4 ingredients in a medium mixing bowl; set aside. Blend
next 6 ingredients together in a large mixing bowl; add flour mixture,
mixing until just blended. Divide batter equally between buttered jars;
wipe rims. Each jar should be slightly less than half full. Place jars on
a jelly-roll pan in the center of the oven; bake at 325 degrees for
40 minutes. Wipe rims; secure lids. Set aside to cool; check for seals.
Makes 3 jars.

For an ooey-gooey treat, give Brownies Baked in a Jar
with whimsical sundae dishes, colorful spoons and a
sampling of ice cream toppings...a welcome treat to
beat the summer heat!

Lemon Cake Baked in a Jar

Old-fashioned long-handled ice cream spoons are the perfect serving utensil to tie on the outside of these cakes...better make it a pair because these treats are meant to be shared.

2-2/3 c. sugar
2/3 c. shortening
4 eggs
1/2 c. lemon juice
1/4 c. water
3 T. lemon zest
1 t. lemon extract

3-1/2 c. all-purpose flour
1 t. baking powder
2 t. baking soda
1 t. salt
7 1-pint, wide-mouth canning
   jars and lids, sterilized

Cream sugar and shortening in a large mixing bowl until light and fluffy; mix in eggs, one at a time, blending well after each addition. Add lemon juice, water, zest and extract; set aside. Combine remaining ingredients in a medium mixing bowl; gradually mix into lemon mixture. Ladle one cup batter into each greased jar; wipe rims. Arrange jars in a jelly-roll pan; bake at 325 degrees until a toothpick inserted in the center removes clean, about 55 minutes. Wipe rims; secure lids and rings. Set aside until cool; check for seals. Keep refrigerated up to 3 months. Makes 7 jars.

Lemon Cake is a refreshing dessert anyone will appreciate! Wrap a jar up with some beach goodies...goggles, sunglasses and a pair of flip-flops inside a colorful bandanna.

July ★ August ★ September

Oh-So-Simple Raspberry Cake

July 31st is National Raspberry Cake Day, so enjoy!

18-1/2 oz. pkg. white cake mix
4 eggs
2/3 c. oil

3-oz. pkg. raspberry gelatin mix
10-oz. pkg. frozen raspberries,
    thawed

Combine ingredients in a mixing bowl; mix 3 minutes with an electric mixer. Spread batter into a greased and floured 13"x9" baking pan; bake at 325 degrees until a toothpick inserted in the center removes clean, about 50 minutes. Cool; frost with cream cheese frosting. Makes 15 to 18 servings.

Cream Cheese Frosting:

3-oz. pkg. cream cheese,
    softened

1 t. vanilla extract
1 T. butter, softened

Blend ingredients together until smooth and creamy.

Make 'em mini! Cut Oh-So-Simple Raspberry Cake into bite-size squares and set inside a retro cake carrier. A toothpick slipped inside each makes for a tasty grab & go snack.

Orchard Road Peach Cobbler

August is National Peach Month!

1/2 c. butter, softened	1 t. salt
1-1/4 c. all-purpose flour	1 c. sugar
2 T. baking powder	1 c. milk

Place butter in a greased 13"x9" glass baking pan; set in oven while preheating to 350 degrees. Combine remaining ingredients in a medium mixing bowl; pour over melted butter. Spoon peaches on top; bake at 350 degrees for 45 minutes. Makes 12 servings.

Peaches:

4 c. peaches, peeled, pitted and sliced	1 t. cinnamon
1/4 c. sugar	1 T. lemon juice

Combine all the ingredients together; set aside for 5 minutes.

Bake this yummy cobbler in a pretty vintage pan...a gift long after the cobbler has been enjoyed. Add a tag that says, "To a real peach!" or "I think you're just peachy!"

July ★ August ★ September

Chocolate-Covered Espresso Beans

A cup of fun to celebrate August as National Coffee Month!

1 c. espresso beans

1 to 1-1/2 c. bittersweet
  chocolate chips, melted

Spread espresso beans about 1/2 inch apart in a wax paper-lined jelly-roll pan; spoon chocolate over the beans. Chill in refrigerator until hard; turn beans over and spread one more time with chocolate. Repeat chilling. Makes one cup.

Spoon flavorful beans into cone-shaped bags used for piping icing, then tie closed with colorful strands of rick-rack. Paired with some fresh biscotti, it makes a delicious early morning treat.

Creamy Caramel Cappuccino

Easily doubled, tripled or quadrupled...the only thing holding you back is the size of your blender!

1/2 c. milk
1/2 c. frozen vanilla yogurt
1 T. caramel ice cream topping

1 pkg. cappuccino-flavored
    instant breakfast drink mix
1 t. vanilla extract

Place all ingredients in a blender; secure lid and blend until smooth. Makes one serving.

Iced Honey Coffee

So refreshing to sip beside a summertime campfire.

2 T. instant coffee granules
1/4 c. boiling water
1/4 c. honey
5 4-inch cinnamon sticks

3/4 c. cold water
3 c. milk
1 c. ice cubes

Dissolve coffee in boiling water; add honey, mixing well. Add one cinnamon stick and cold water; stir and set aside. Fill 4 tall serving glasses with ice; discard cinnamon stick and add 1/4 cup coffee mixture to each glass. Fill with milk; add one cinnamon stick to each glass. Serves 4.

July ★ August ★ September

Ginger Spice & Everything Nice Muffin Mix

Friendship Day falls on the first Sunday in August…take time to appreciate friends near & dear.

1-3/4 c. all-purpose flour
2-1/2 T. sugar
1 T. baking powder
1/2 t. baking soda
1 t. cinnamon

1/2 t. nutmeg
1/4 t. ground ginger
1/4 t. ground cloves
1/2 t. salt

Combine all ingredients; spoon into an airtight container. Seal; attach instructions.

Instructions:

Place mix in a large mixing bowl; stir in 1/4 cup melted butter, one egg, one teaspoon vanilla extract and one cup milk. Mix well; fill paper-lined or greased muffin cups 2/3 full with batter. Bake at 400 degrees for 15 minutes. Makes one dozen.

Slip this mix inside a pretty copper watering can for a friend who loves gardening or a retro sewing tin for a friend who loves embroidery. Either way, it's a tasty gift that shows you care.

Cinnamon & Sugar Crispies

Don't forget your little neighborhood friends...deliver bags of warm crispies for their morning snacks!

10 8-inch flour tortillas   1/3 c. sugar
3 c. oil   1 T. cinnamon

Cut each tortilla into 8 wedges; set aside. Heat oil to 400 degrees in a deep skillet; fry 10 wedges at a time, turning occasionally until golden, about 30 to 40 seconds. Drain on paper towels. Place sugar and cinnamon in a large plastic bag; add warm tortilla wedges, shaking until well coated. Makes about 6-1/2 dozen.

Wrap Cinnamon & Sugar Crispies inside a vintage-pattern tea towel...another sweet gift for Friendship Day.

July ★ August ★ September

Friendship Bread

An old favorite everyone has fun trying.

1 c. all-purpose flour   1 c. milk
1 c. sugar   1-gal. plastic zipping bag

Starter:
Combine ingredients in a glass bowl; mix well with a wooden spoon. Pour into bag. Squeeze every day for 17 days; do nothing on day 18; squeeze on days 19, 20 and 21; add same ingredients to bag on day 22; squeeze on days 23, 24, 25 and 26; add same ingredients again on day 27, squeezing to mix. There are now about 4 cups starter. Give 2 friends each one cup starter with the following instructions attached. Place one cup starter in another bag for yourself; use remaining to make Friendship Bread.

Instructions:

Day 1: you receive starter-do not refrigerate; the batter will thicken, bubble and ferment. You may let air out of bag; reseal.

Days 2, 3, 4 and 5: squeeze the bag.

Day 6: add one cup sugar, one cup all-purpose flour, one cup milk; squeeze the bag.

Days 7, 8 and 9: squeeze the bag.

Day 10: pour mixture into a large glass mixing bowl; add one cup all-purpose flour, one cup sugar and one cup milk, stirring with a wooden spoon. Pour 4, one-cup starters into separate one-gallon plastic zipping bags. To remaining mix in bowl, add 3/4 cup oil, one cup sugar, one teaspoon vanilla extract, 3 eggs, 1/2 teaspoon salt, 2 teaspoons cinnamon, 2 cups all-purpose flour, 1/2 cup milk, 1/2 teaspoon baking soda, 3.4-oz. pkg. vanilla instant pudding mix and 1-1/2 teaspoons baking powder. Mix well. Divide and pour evenly into 2 greased 9"x5" loaf pans; sprinkle lightly with cinnamon and sugar. Bake at 325 degrees for one hour. Makes 2 loaves.

Whoopie Pies

A recipe sure to guarantee smiles, which is good since the 2nd week of August is National Smile Week!

2-1/4 c. all-purpose flour	2/3 c. shortening
1/2 c. baking cocoa	2 eggs
1-1/2 t. baking soda	1 t. vanilla extract
1-1/4 t. cream of tartar	1 c. milk
1-1/4 c. sugar	

Combine first 4 ingredients; set aside. Cream sugar and shortening until fluffy in a large mixing bowl; add eggs and vanilla, mixing well. Alternately mix in flour mixture and milk; blend until just combined. Drop by tablespoonfuls onto greased baking sheets; bake at 350 degrees for 8 to 10 minutes. Transfer to wire racks to cool completely. Spread heaping teaspoonfuls of filling on flat sides of half the cookies; top each with another half, making a sandwich. Wrap in plastic wrap; freeze until firm. Makes about 2-1/2 dozen.

Filling:

5 T. all-purpose flour	1 c. sugar
1 c. milk	1/4 t. salt
1 c. shortening	1-1/2 t. vanilla extract
1/2 c. butter, softened	

Combine flour and milk in a small saucepan; heat over medium heat until thick, stirring constantly. Set aside to cool to room temperature. Cream shortening, butter, sugar, salt and vanilla together; mix in milk mixture. Blend until stiff peaks form.

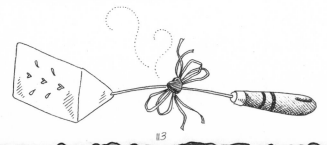

July ★ August ★ September

Waffly-Good Snack Mix

This yummy mix can be made anytime...try substituting candy corn in the Autumn for the candy-coated chocolates.

4 c. waffle-shaped crispy cereal
1/2 c. peanuts
1/3 c. raisins

2 T. butter, melted
1/2 c. candy-coated chocolates

Gently toss the first 3 ingredients together in a large bowl; drizzle butter on top, mixing to coat. Spread mixture in an ungreased jelly-roll pan; bake at 350 degrees for 10 minutes, stirring after 5 minutes. Cool; mix in candy-coated chocolates. Store in an airtight container. Makes 5-1/2 cups.

Children's sand pails can be found at antique shops. Filled with a bag of this mix and a new sand shovel for scooping, it's an ideal hostess gift for a summertime get-together.

Buttery Pistachio Brittle

Make on a breezy day with low to no humidity...better yet, turn up the air conditioner and pretend it's Christmas in July!

2 c. sugar
1 c. corn syrup
1/2 c. water
1 c. butter

2 c. salted shelled pistachios
1 t. baking soda
1 t. vanilla extract

Combine first 3 ingredients in a heavy 3-quart saucepan; heat over low heat until sugar dissolves and mixture comes to a rolling boil, stirring occasionally. Add butter; continue heating until mixture reaches the soft-crack stage, 270 to 289 degrees on a candy thermometer, stirring occasionally. Stir in pistachios; continue heating, stirring constantly, until mixture reaches the hard-crack stage, 290 to 310 degrees on a candy thermometer. Remove from heat; carefully stir in baking soda and vanilla. Pour mixture in 2 buttered jelly-roll pans; spread with forks until about 1/4-inch thick. Cool completely; break into pieces and store in an airtight container. Makes about 2 pounds.

Delivered in a clever container, Buttery Pistachio Brittle is a great way to say "I'm nuts about you!" Use decoupage medium to secure nuts and bolts to the flat lid of a jar; let dry. Use a clear epoxy coating, and following manufacturer's instructions, apply coating to lid. Allow to dry, attach to mix-filled jar.

July ⋆ August ⋆ September

Mocha-Mint Meltaway Mix

Be prepared to have the empty jar returned to be filled over and over again!

2 c. rich hot cocoa mix   1/4 t. peppermint extract
1/4 c. instant coffee granules   1/4 t. vanilla powder

Process ingredients together in a blender until powdered; spoon into an airtight jar. Attach instructions. Makes 2-1/4 cups.

Instructions:

Add 3 tablespoons mix to one cup hot milk or water; stir until dissolved. Makes one cup.

a little
something
for you!

This plain brown lunch bag is anything but plain!
Place a jar of Mocha-Mint Meltaway Mix inside the
bag; set aside. Cut a flower shape from felt, stitch a
button to the center, then use hot glue to secure the
flower to a spring-type clothespin. When glue is dry,
fold the sack top down and clip on flower.

Terrific Truffle Cake Mix

An oh-so-sweet September 28th Good Neighbor Day treat!

3 c. all-purpose flour
3 c. sugar
1 t. baking soda

1/2 c. baking cocoa
1/2 t. vanilla powder

Combine all ingredients; place in a plastic zipping bag. Attach instructions.

Instructions:

Cream 3/4 cup softened butter; add 5 eggs, one at a time, mixing well after each addition. Add one cup milk; mix well. Add mix; blend for 3 minutes. Pour into a greased 9-cup Bundt® pan; bake at 325 degrees for 60 to 70 minutes, or until a toothpick inserted in the center removes clean. Cool 25 minutes; remove from pan and cool completely. Makes 15 to 18 servings.

Make a cone shape from pretty scrapbook paper, glue in place. Punch a hole in each side of the cone and slide ribbon or rick-rack through to make a handle. Slipped over a doorknob, it's sure to be a welcome Good Neighbor Day surprise!

July ★ August ★ September

Autumn Lunch Box

Give a plain tin lunch box a pick-me-up with a leaf stencil and some acrylic paint!

tin lunch box
spray primer
assorted acrylic paints

oak leaf stencil
sponge
clear acrylic sealer

Wash and dry lunch box; apply primer, let dry and add 2 coats acrylic paint. When paint has dried, lay stencil on lunch box and sponge paint inside stencil. Gently remove stencil and repeat in a random pattern. When stencil paint is thoroughly dry, top lunch box with 2 or 3 coats of sealer.

Terrific for school lunches, of course, but this Autumn Lunch Box is also perfect for filling with snacks and taking to a school ball game.

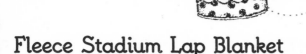

Fleece Stadium Lap Blanket

September also signals kick-off time, so cheer on your favorite team while keeping warm under this easy-to-stitch stadium blanket.

2-1/2 yds. of 2 colors of fleece   measuring tape
rotary cutter or scissors   sewing machine & thread
cutting mat

Begin by cutting seventeen, 10-1/2 inch squares from the first color fleece and eighteen, 10-1/2 inch squares from the second color fleece. Alternating colors, overlap each square 1/4 inch and zigzag stitch 7 squares together to make a row. For the second row, be sure to alternate the order of colors used in the first row. Repeat making 4 more rows. Matching along the row edges, sew strips together.

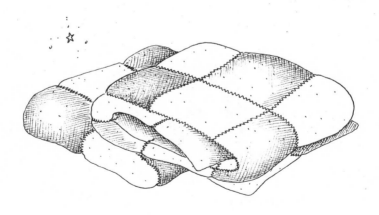

A fleece blanket is a perfect way to keep Grandma & Grandpa warm during football games...give along with a hot water bottle to keep them extra warm & cozy!

July ★ August ★ September

Banana Cupcake Mix

The International Banana Festival is September 21...be prepared!

1 c. all-purpose flour
1/3 c. plus 3 T. sugar
2-1/2 t. baking powder

1/2 t. salt
1 c. whole-bran

Combine ingredients; place in a plastic zipping bag. Seal;
attach instructions.

Instructions:

Blend one egg and 1/3 cup milk together; gradually stir in mix. Fill
12 greased or paper-lined muffin cups half full with batter; center one
banana slice into each muffin cup. Fill to 3/4 full with remaining
batter; sprinkle 2 tablespoons brown sugar evenly over muffins. Bake
at 400 degrees for 15 minutes. Makes one dozen.

A few bags of Banana Cupcake Mix and some mini
baking tools will be a sweet gift for a young baker.
Try tucking the goodies inside the pockets of a
kid-size kitchen apron.

Nutty Banana Bread Baked in a Jar

Treat all your co-workers…bring in a "bunch" of banana bread jars!

2/3 c. shortening
2-2/3 c. sugar
4 eggs
2 c. bananas, mashed
2/3 c. water
3-1/3 c. all-purpose flour
1/2 t. baking powder
2 t. baking soda

1 t. salt
1 t. cinnamon
1 t. ground cloves
2/3 c. chopped pecans
8 1-pint, wide-mouth canning
   jars and lids, sterilized

Cream shortening with sugar in a large mixing bowl until light and fluffy; blend in eggs, bananas and water. Set aside. Combine flour, baking powder, baking soda, salt, cinnamon and cloves; blend into egg mixture. Fold in pecans; fill jars half full with batter. Wipe rims; arrange on a jelly-roll pan. Bake at 325 degrees for 45 minutes; wipe rims. Secure lids and rings; set aside to cool. Check for seals; sealed jars may be stored in a cool, dry cupboard for up to 6 weeks. Makes 8 jars.

Give jars of banana bread inside a Banana Split Kit. Just fill a decorated bag with mix, banana split toppings, bananas and whipped topping. Give with directions to slice banana bread then pile on the ice cream and toppings…yum!

July ✦ August ✦ September

Lovin' Raisin Loaf

The first Sunday after Labor Day is Grandparents' Day. Here's an
old-fashioned treat all grandparents will enjoy!

1 c. raisins
2 c. all-purpose flour, divided
2 t. baking powder
1/4 t. baking soda
1 t. salt

1/3 c. sugar
2 c. bran cereal
1 egg, beaten
1-1/2 c. buttermilk
1/4 c. shortening, melted

Toss raisins and 1/4 cup flour together until well coated; set aside.
Combine remaining flour, baking powder, baking soda, salt and sugar
together in a large mixing bowl; add raisin mixture and cereal. Set
aside. Whisk egg, buttermilk and shortening together; mix into flour
mixture until just moistened. Spread into a greased 9"x5" loaf pan;
bake at 350 degrees until a toothpick inserted in the center removes
clean, about one hour. Makes 8 servings.

A retro breadbox is the best way to share a warm
loaf of Lovin' Raisin Loaf. Add a crock
of butter too!

Hug-in-a-Jug Butterscotch Brownie Mix

OK, a hug-in-a-jar, but that doesn't rhyme...however, this Butterscotch Brownie Mix tripled could fit in a jug!

1/2 c. flaked coconut, packed
3/4 c. chopped pecans
2 c. brown sugar, packed
2 c. all-purpose flour

1-1/2 T. baking powder
1/4 t. salt
1 c. butterscotch chips

Layer first 6 ingredients in the order listed in a one-quart, wide-mouth jar; pack each layer firmly before adding the next ingredient. Place butterscotch chips in a plastic zipping bag. Secure lid; tie on plastic bag and instructions.

Instructions:

Place mix in a large mixing bowl, setting bag to the side; toss gently to mix. Add 3/4 cup softened butter, 2 beaten eggs and 2 teaspoons vanilla extract; mix well. Spread in a greased 13"x9" baking pan; bake at 375 degrees for 25 minutes. Sprinkle with butterscotch chips; cool and cut into bars to serve. Makes 2 dozen.

Moms sending the kids off on their first day of school could probably use a friend! Attach a phone-shaped tag to this mix inviting her to call and chat any time.

July ★ August ★ September

Applesauce Bread & Muffin Mix

A handy mix to keep stocked in the pantry.

4 c. sugar
7 c. all-purpose flour
4 t. salt
4 t. baking powder
2 t. baking soda

2-1/2 t. cinnamon
2 t. nutmeg
1 t. vanilla powder
2 c. shortening

Combine dry ingredients in a large mixing bowl; cut in shortening with a pastry cutter until coarse crumbs form. Store in an airtight container in a cool, dry cupboard up to 4 months. Attach instructions. Makes 13-1/2 cups.

Applesauce Bread:

Combine 3-1/2 cups mix with 2 eggs and one cup applesauce; spread into a greased and floured 9"x5" loaf pan. Bake at 350 degrees for 40 to 50 minutes. Serves 8.

Applesauce Muffins:

Prepare as above; fill greased muffin cups 3/4 full with batter. Bake at 350 degrees for 20 to 30 minutes. Makes one dozen.

Fill a pantry jar with this mix and tie on an
old-fashioned measuring cup with an
apple-green handle!

Back-to-School Apple Cake Mix

What a nice treat to drop off for your favorite teacher on their first day back...tuck in a red, shiny apple too!

3 c. all-purpose flour
1-1/2 c. sugar
1-1/2 t. baking soda
1 t. vanilla powder

2 t. cinnamon
1/4 t. nutmeg
1 c. chopped walnuts
1/2 c. raisins

Combine all ingredients in a medium mixing bowl; place into an airtight container. Attach instructions.

Instructions:

Place mix in a large mixing bowl; form a well in the center. Add 1-1/2 cups oil, 3 eggs and 3 cups cored, peeled and chopped apples; stir until combined. Pour into a greased Bundt® pan; bake at 350 degrees until a toothpick inserted in the center removes clean, about 60 to 70 minutes. Cool; remove from pan. Makes 15 servings.

You're sure to get an A+ when the teacher finds Back-to-School Apple Cake Mix in a chalkboard-inspired bag! Use white dimensional paint to write a message on a black gift bag; let dry. Set the mix inside and fold over the top. Punch 2 holes in the bag fold and insert a pencil through the holes.

July ★ August ★ September

Stadium Mix

*Fun to rename depending on the game...Penguins' Party Picks, Chief
Wahoo's Nibbles or Titan's Tidbits to name a few!*

3 c. puffed corn cereal
2 c. bite-size corn and rice cereal
   squares
2-1/2 c. mini pretzel sticks
1-1/2 c. mixed nuts
3 T. butter

1 T. Worcestershire sauce
1-1/2 t. chili powder
1 t. garlic powder
3 c. bite-size cheese cracker
   squares

Combine first 4 ingredients in a large roaster; set aside. Add butter,
Worcestershire sauce, chili powder and garlic powder to a small
saucepan; heat over low heat until butter melts. Drizzle over cereal
mixture; toss gently to coat. Bake at 300 degrees for 30 minutes,
stirring every 10 minutes; add cheese crackers, tossing to mix. Spread
mix out on aluminum foil; cool. Store in an airtight container up to
5 days. Makes 11 cups.

Scoop Stadium Mix into a thermos sporting a favorite
pro football team...the thermos will come in handy
long after the snack's been enjoyed!

Game-Time Popcorn Seasoning Mix

Sprinkle over hot, buttered popcorn for a spicy half-time snack.

1 t. salt
1 t. chili powder
1 t. garlic powder

1 t. cumin
1 T. dried, minced onion
1/8 t. cayenne pepper

Combine ingredients; store in an airtight container. Makes about 1/8 cup.

for a poppin' good time!

Make lots of this mix and spoon into brightly colored glassine bags secured with a pipe cleaner and a tag that reads, "For a poppin' good time!"

July ★ August ★ September

Beef & Barley Stew Mix

So nice to have on hand for those crisp autumn evenings.

1 T. dried basil
1-1/2 t. dried oregano
1-1/2 t. pepper
3/4 c. beef bouillon granules

3 c. pearled barley
3 c. dried split green peas
6 bay leaves
6 plastic zipping bags

Combine first 3 ingredients; divide equally into 6 portions, spooning each portion into a plastic zipping bag. Add 2 tablespoons bouillon to each bag; spoon 1/2 cup pearled barley and 1/2 cup split peas into each bag. Place one bay leaf into each bag; seal. Attach instructions. Makes 6 bags.

Instructions:

Heat 2 tablespoons oil in a large stockpot; brown one pound beef stew cubes. Add 6 cups water and one package Beef & Barley Stew Mix; bring to a boil. Reduce heat; cover and simmer for 45 minutes. Add one cup sliced celery, one cup sliced carrots and 3 peeled and sliced potatoes; cover and simmer for one additional hour. Discard bay leaf before serving. Serves 4.

Since Beef & Barley Stew Mix makes 6 individual bags, it's a great idea for a college care package. Just for fun, put all 6 bags into a megaphone sporting school colors!

Cozy One-Cup Vegetable Soup Mix

Send packets of this mix to college students along with a hometown mug to remind them they have a whole community rooting for them!

1-1/2 T. vegetable soup mix
3 T. instant rice, uncooked

1 t. chicken bouillon granules
1/2 t. onion powder

Combine ingredients; place in a small airtight jar or plastic zipping bag. Secure lid or seal; attach instructions.

Instructions:

Place soup mix in a microwave-safe mug; add one cup water, stirring to mix. Microwave on high setting for 1-1/2 minutes; stir. Microwave 30 to 45 additional seconds. Cover and let stand 5 minutes. Makes one serving.

Another easy mix for those late night dorm study sessions. Place mix in a colorful bag and fold the top of the bag over. To secure, use a hole punch and make 2 holes near the top, then just slide a college pennant stick through the holes.

July ★ August ★ September

Fleece Hat

Keep warm in the crisp autumn weather with this simple-to-make hat that's wonderfully warm and machine washable!

24"x14" fleece fabric panel
soft tape measure
scissors

sewing machine
needle & thread
pom-pom

To determine the exact width of the fleece panel, measure the circumference of your head above your ears. Add 1/2 inch and cut. The length for an adult hat is about 13 inches; for a child-size hat, about 10 inches. Form a tube by bringing long edges together, right-side together. Sew long edge using 1/4-inch seam allowance. To close top, center seam on hat and sew 1/4-inch seam across end. Fold up open end 3 inches and stitch along edge. Turn hat right-side out. Thread needle and slip through one corner, and then through the other; pull thread tightly so the corners come together in the center. Knot thread, then stitch pom-pom in place.

Not only will the hat be a terrific gift, tuck a packet of cider mix inside for an extra surprise!

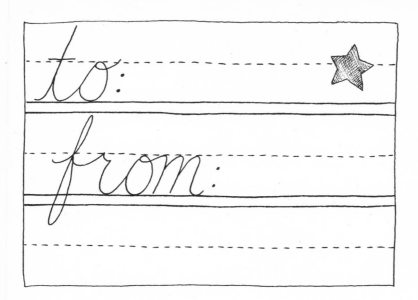

to:

from:

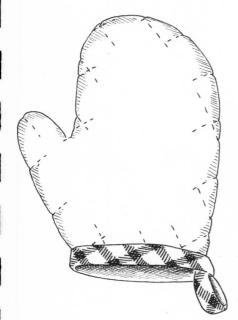

Don't forget to write
the instructions
on the back!

131

Feel free to copy these tags and use colored pens to give them some zing!

a little gift from:

October
November
December

October ✷ November ✷ December

Cider Syrup

Served over a stack of hot cakes or waffles, this is a yummy addition to any autumn breakfast table!

1 c. sugar
2 T. cornstarch
1/2 t. pumpkin pie spice

2 c. apple cider
2 T. lemon juice
1/3 c. butter

Place first 3 ingredients in a saucepan; stir in apple cider and lemon juice. Heat over medium heat, stirring constantly until mixture thickens and boils; boil for one minute. Remove from heat; stir in butter. Makes about 2 cups.

While this sweet & spicy Cider Syrup is still warm, pour into a thermos and pack inside a vintage-style lunch tin with some pancake mix or fresh biscuits.

Cinnamon Pancakes in a Jar

Perfect paired with Cider Syrup...what a combination!

3 c. all-purpose flour   4-1/2 t. cinnamon
3 T. sugar   1 t. salt
2 T. baking powder

Gently toss all ingredients together; spoon into a one-quart jar. Secure lid; attach instructions.

Instructions:

Whisk 3/4 cup milk, one egg and 2 tablespoons oil together in a medium mixing bowl; add 1-1/3 cups mix, stirring until just moistened. Pour by 1/4 cupfuls onto a hot, greased skillet; heat until bubbles form along the edge. Flip and heat until both sides are golden. Makes 10.

A simple bittersweet twig wreath slipped around the middle of the jar dresses it up nicely for gift-giving!

Molasses-Pumpkin Pie

Make an extra pie crust and cut out leaf shapes using mini cookie cutters, arrange around pie crust edges, "gluing" in place with a mixture of egg white and water...bake as usual.

3/4 c. sugar
1 T. all-purpose flour
1/2 t. salt
1 t. ground ginger
1/2 t. cinnamon
1/4 t. ground cloves

1/4 t. nutmeg
1/4 c. molasses
2 c. canned pumpkin, mashed
3 eggs
1 c. evaporated milk
9-inch pie crust

Blend first 7 ingredients together in a medium mixing bowl; mix in the next 3 ingredients. Stir in milk; spread into pie crust. Bake at 400 degrees until a knife inserted in the center removes clean, about 40 minutes. Cool. Makes 8 servings.

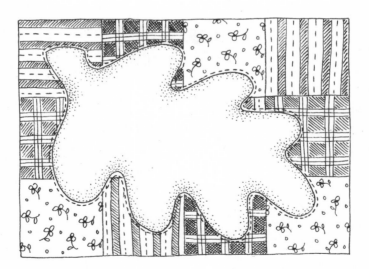

Nestle a warm Molasses-Pumpkin Pie inside a red and orange berry wreath...it'll be a perfect harvest welcome wreath long after the pie's gone!

Slow-Cooker Pumpkin Bread in Jars

Decorate jars to look like pumpkins...happy October!

1 c. all-purpose flour
1-1/2 t. baking powder
2 t. pumpkin pie spice
1/2 c. brown sugar, packed
2 T. oil
2 eggs

1/2 c. canned pumpkin
1/4 c. raisins
2 1/2-pint, wide-mouth
   canning jars and lids,
   sterilized

Combine first 3 ingredients in a small mixing bowl; set aside. Blend brown sugar and oil together in a medium mixing bowl; mix in eggs and pumpkin. Gradually add flour mixture until just combined; fold in raisins. Divide and pour equally into 2 greased and floured canning jars; cover jars tightly with greased aluminum foil. Line bottom of 4-quart slow cooker with several loosely crumpled balls of aluminum foil; arrange jars on top. Cover and heat on high setting for 1-1/2 to 2 hours or until a toothpick inserted in the center removes clean. Remove jars from cooker; set aside 10 minutes. Remove bread from jars; cool completely on a wire rack. Makes 2 jars.

Slide these
1/2-pint jars into
replica paper maché
Jack-'0-Lantern
baskets for
a hauntingly
good gift!

Shortcake Sweeties

For Sweetest Day, the 3rd Saturday in October, make these extra special by dipping half of each cookie in melted bittersweet chocolate or drizzle the top of each with melted raspberry chips.

1 c. butter
3/4 c. powdered sugar
1 t. vanilla extract

2 c. all-purpose flour
1/2 t. salt

Cream butter, sugar and vanilla until light and fluffy; blend in flour and salt on low speed of an electric mixer. Wrap dough in plastic wrap; chill until firm, at least 2 hours. Roll out dough on a lightly floured surface to 1/8 to 1/4-inch thickness; cut into hearts using a 2-inch heart-shaped cookie cutter. Arrange on ungreased baking sheets; refrigerate for 30 minutes. Lightly pierce tops of cookies with fork tines; bake at 300 degrees until golden, about 18 minutes. Cool; store in an airtight container up to one week. Makes about 2 dozen.

Shortcake Sweeties become a real gift from
the heart when served on a graceful pink
glass cake stand.

"Happy Sweetest Day!" Hearts

A fun treat for all the young sweeties in the neighborhood or at home. Wrap individually in red cellophane and pile in a basket.

10 c. popped popcorn   red food coloring
3 T. butter   red sanding sugar
10-oz. pkg. marshmallows

Spread popcorn in a greased 13"x9" baking pan; keep warm in a 300-degree oven. Melt butter and marshmallows together in a large heavy saucepan over low heat; stir until smooth. Mix in food coloring to desired tint; gradually add popcorn, stirring until coated. Cool 10 to 15 minutes; press into individual one-cup buttered heart-shaped molds. Cool; remove from molds. Sprinkle with sugar. Makes 10.

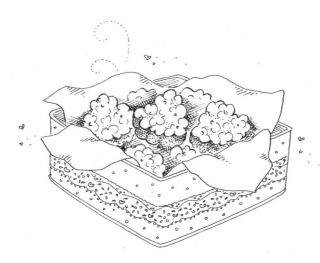

Recycle a tin candy box by decoupaging it with pretty scrapbook paper and "lace" stickers. Line the tin with raspberry colored tissue paper and fill with "Happy Sweetest Day!" Hearts.

Sweet & Salty Bars

Give 'em a giggle when handing out these goodies...kids big and little will love the clever packaging!

6 c. marshmallows, divided
1-1/2 c. chocolate chips
5 T. butter
1/4 c. corn syrup

1-1/2 t. vanilla extract
6 c. graham cracker cereal mix
2 c. pretzels, coarsely broken

Melt 5 cups marshmallows, chocolate chips and butter with corn syrup in a heavy 3-quart saucepan over low heat; stir until smooth. Remove from heat; add remaining ingredients, stirring to coat. Spread in a buttered 13"x9" baking pan; cool one hour. Cut into bars. Makes 2 dozen.

A treat and a costume all in one! Once Sweet & Salty Bars are wrapped and inside a brown lunch bag, fold the top down, tie on a rubber nose and top with a witches' hat.

Pretzels

It's October...Happy National Pretzel Month! Have fun shaping dough into letters, twists or standard pretzel shapes!

1 pkg. active dry yeast
1 c. warm water
2 T. oil
1/2 t. salt

2-3/4 c. all-purpose flour, divided
4 c. water
2 T. baking soda
3 T. coarse salt

Sprinkle yeast over water; set aside 10 minutes. Add oil, salt and 1-1/2 cups flour; mix well. Stir in remaining flour; knead for 5 minutes. Set dough aside for one hour. Divide into 12 equal portions; roll into balls. Set aside for 15 minutes. Shape into desired shapes; let rise for 30 minutes. Pour water and baking soda into a large saucepan; bring to a boil. Add pretzels to boiling water; boil for one minute. Arrange on greased baking sheets; sprinkle with coarse salt. Bake at 475 degrees for 12 minutes. Makes one dozen.

Paint and stencil a Shaker box with primitive fall designs...choose pumpkins, stars, a checkerboard border and a crackle finish to make the box look old. Filled with homemade pretzels, this is one treat sure to be enjoyed!

Blackberry Bog Nog

It's all in the name...for Halloween it's Blackberry Bog Nog, wait another month and rename Pilgrim's Pride. No matter when it's served, this eggnog is always good!

4 egg yolks, beaten
1-3/4 c. milk
1/3 c. sugar
1/2 t. nutmeg

1 c. whipping cream
2 t. vanilla extract
1-1/2 c. blackberries

Combine egg yolks, milk, sugar and nutmeg in a saucepan; heat and stir over medium heat until mixture coats a metal spoon. Remove from heat; place pan in a bowl of ice water. Stir for 2 minutes; mix in cream and vanilla. Cover with plastic wrap and chill for at least 4 hours, or up to 24 hours. Place blackberries into a large glass pitcher; pour nog on top. Serve immediately. Serves 8.

Pour this delicious nog into milk bottles, add the lid and top each with a berry-colored square of tissue paper secured with jute...set inside a wire carrier for delivering to friends & neighbors.

Marshmallow-Caramel Apples

It's just not October without these chewy, sweet treats!

14-oz. pkg. caramels,
   unwrapped
1 c. mini marshmallows
1 T. water

5 to 6 6-inch wooden skewers
5 to 6 tart apples, washed and
   patted dry

Combine caramels, marshmallows and water in heavy saucepan; heat over medium heat until caramels melt, stirring constantly. Cool slightly. Insert skewers into apples; dip in caramel mixture. Place on a buttered wax paper-lined baking sheet; refrigerate until firm. Makes 5 to 6.

After wrapping each apple in cellophane, nestle inside
a small orange gift sack. Add a pumpkin face to the
sack using a black permanent marker, then gather the
sack around the apple stick
and tie on green curling ribbon.

October ★ November ★ December

Potpourri Pie

Scent with apple and spice potpourri for a fall treat to be enjoyed by all.

2 c. all-purpose flour
1 c. salt
1 c. water
1 pot pie tin
1 egg white

1/8 t. cinnamon
1/8 t. ground cloves
potpourri
hot glue gun & glue

Combine flour, salt and water; mix until smooth. Roll out into a 1/4-inch thick rectangle; cut out six, 1/2-inch wide strips. Weave the strips, 3 in each direction; place on top of an upside-down pot pie tin, trimming edges even with bottom rim of pie tin. Set aside. Cut one additional strip of dough long enough to cover the rim of the pie tin; arrange around strips, covering edges. Wet edges of pie lattices with water so they will adhere to bottom of pie rim edging. Brush dough with egg white; sprinkle with cinnamon and cloves. Place pie tin with dough on an aluminum foil-lined baking sheet; bake at 325 degrees until golden, about 25 to 30 minutes. Cool; gently separate crust from pie tin. Fill tin with potpourri; arrange crust on top, gluing in place with hot glue. Makes one.

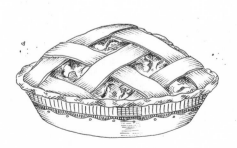

Invite friends over to make these fragrant "pies"
assembly-line style! It's such fun to spend an
afternoon with the girls crafting away!

Face Paint

Easy to apply and wipes right off with cold cream!

1 t. cornstarch
1/2 t. cold cream

1/2 t. water
food coloring

Combine ingredients together; mix well. Store in an airtight container.
Makes 2 teaspoons.

Shimmering Body Glitter

Star and moon shaped glitter is fun to add for a certain spooky night.

1 T. aloe vera gel
food coloring

glitter assortment

Combine aloe vera gel and food coloring until desired tint is achieved;
gradually sprinkle in glitter and mix until desired sparkle is achieved.
Store in an airtight container. Makes one tablespoon.

Face Paint is ideal for little trick-or-treaters...it lets
them use their imagination and they can easily see
what's around them as they go from house to house.

Crazy Cauldron Snack Mix

*Let the kids try to guess what their ingredient
really is before they add it to the cauldron!*

1/2 c. blood droplets (red cinnamon candies)
1/2 c. petrified cat eyes (blanched almonds)
1/2 c. cat claws (sunflower kernels)
1 c. chicken toenails (candy corn)
1 c. colored flies (candy-coated chocolates)

1 c. butterfly wings (corn chips)
1 c. ants (raisins)
1 c. glowworms (cheese curls)
1 c. cobwebs (shredded wheat crackers, coarsely broken)
1 c. snake eyes (peanuts)
1 c. bat bones (potato sticks)
1 c. monster molars (mini marshmallows)

Combine all ingredients in a large mixing bowl or clean, plastic cauldron; gently toss to mix. Makes 10-1/2 cups.

Place each ingredient in its own paper lunch bag
stencilled with black cats, ghosts or bats, then tie
closed with a glow-in-the-dark yo-yo.

Dirt Cups

Layer in clear cups and serve with "tombstone" spoons...oval-shaped shortbread cookies will do.

2 c. milk
3.9-oz. pkg. instant chocolate
   pudding mix
8-oz. container frozen whipped
   topping, thawed

16-oz. pkg. chocolate sandwich
   cookies, crushed and divided
4 9-oz. clear plastic cups
Garnish: gummi worms, gummi
   frogs, peanuts and granola

Whisk milk and pudding mix together until well blended; let stand for 5 minutes. Fold in whipped topping and half the crushed cookies; set aside. Spoon one tablespoon remaining crushed cookies into each cup; fill 3/4 full with pudding. Sprinkle with remaining crushed cookies; refrigerate at least one hour or until ready to serve. Garnish with gummi creatures, peanut "rocks" and granola "sand." Makes 4 servings.

Kids will giggle when they see these! Give Dirt Cups wrapped in cellophane...keep each securely closed by tying with raffia and securing with a plastic spider ring!

October ★ November ★ December

Polka Dot Pizza Pals

A fun snack to make with groups of kids and adults.

10-oz. can refrigerated pizza
    dough
1/4 c. diced pepperoni

1/2 c. pizza sauce
1 c. shredded mozzarella cheese
1 c. French-fried onions

Roll out dough on a lightly floured surface into a 12"x8" rectangle;
sprinkle pepperoni evenly over the top, gently pressing into dough.
Cut dough into desired shapes using cookie cutters; reroll dough scraps
and continue cutting out desired shapes. Arrange shapes on a greased
baking sheet; bake at 425 degrees for 7 minutes. Spread with pizza
sauce and sprinkle with cheese; bake 6 additional minutes. Top with
French-fried onions; bake a final 2 minutes. Makes 4 to 6 servings.

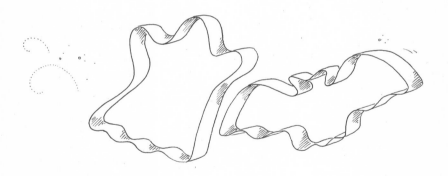

October is National Pizza Month so treat little goblins
to a spooky pizza dinner. When making Polka Dot
Pizza Pals, cut the dough using Halloween cookie
cutters.

Pizza Popcorn Spice Mix

*Sprinkle this mix over 2 quarts popped popcorn for a
real pizza-pleasing taste!*

2 T. grated Parmesan cheese   1 t. garlic powder
2 T. spaghetti sauce mix   1 t. Italian seasoning

Blend all 4 ingredients together until powdered; spoon into an airtight
container. Makes about 1/4 cup.

Cut a "window" from a lunch bag using an autumn
leaf cookie cutter as the stencil. Glue a square of
cellophane inside the bag over the cut-out, then line
the bag with orange tissue paper to show through the
"window." Slip in the Pizza Popcorn Spice Mix and
give to a pizza-loving friend!

October ★ November ★ December

Cheddar Crackers

Vote's in...fill a bowl with these to share while watching the returns or for snacking on while working the Election Day church supper.

2 c. shredded sharp Cheddar
   cheese
1/2 c. butter, softened

1-1/2 c. all-purpose flour
1/2 t. garlic salt
1/4 t. cayenne pepper

Combine cheese and butter in a large mixing bowl; blend with an electric mixer until well mixed. Add remaining ingredients; mix well. Divide dough in half; shape each into a 7-inch long roll. Wrap in plastic wrap; refrigerate for at least one hour. Slice into 1/4-inch thick rounds; arrange on an ungreased baking sheet. Bake at 350 degrees for 15 minutes; cool on a wire rack. Store in an airtight container in the refrigerator for up to one week or freeze up to 3 months. Makes about 4-1/2 dozen.

Heap Cheddar Crackers inside a flag-inspired bowl. Use a foam brush to paint the outside of a wooden bowl blue; allow to dry. Stencil on white stars using acrylic paint. Apply 3 coats of acrylic sealer to protect paint and let dry thoroughly. Line bowl with a cheery red cloth and fill with crackers...easy!

Zesty Mozzarella Cheese Bites

A tasty take-along Election Night nibbler.

16-oz. pkg. mozzarella cheese
1/4 c. roasted garlic oil
2 t. balsamic vinegar

2 T. fresh basil, chopped
1 T. whole mixed peppercorns,
    coarsely ground

Cube cheese into 1/2-inch cubes; place in a medium mixing bowl. Set aside. Whisk remaining ingredients together; pour over cheese cubes. Toss to coat; cover and refrigerate up to 3 days. Makes 14 servings.

Fill a wire basket with a jar of Zesty Mozzarella Cheese Bites, crackers, fresh vegetables and dip. Weave a red, white & blue ribbon through the wire to add patriotic flair!

What-a-Parade Cocoa Mix

Thanksgiving Day is filled from beginning to end and this mix makes enough to serve all day long, from early morning parade watchers to late night football game fans.

1/2 c. sugar	1/4 c. baking cocoa
2 T. whole almonds	1/2 t. vanilla powder
1-oz. sq. bittersweet baking chocolate, chopped	1 t. cinnamon
	1/2 t. ground cloves

Place sugar and almonds in a food processor; process until almonds are finely ground. Add remaining ingredients; process until mixture is finely ground. Store in an airtight container; attach instructions. Makes one cup.

Instructions:

Add one tablespoon mix to one cup hot milk; whisk until frothy. Makes one serving.

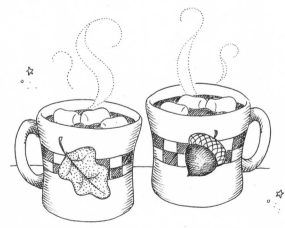

For a parade-day gift, fill a jar with cocoa mix and slip inside a bag along with mugs, the remote control and a copy of the television guide!

Brown Sugar Granola

Decorate an empty cardboard oat canister and fill with this yummy snack...so handy to nibble on while traveling to visit family.

2 T. butter
1/4 c. corn syrup
1/4 c. honey
2-3/4 c. quick-cooking oats, uncooked

1/2 c. sliced almonds
1/2 c. brown sugar, packed
1-1/2 t. cinnamon
1/2 c. flaked coconut, toasted

Melt butter with corn syrup and honey in a small saucepan; set aside. Combine remaining ingredients except coconut in a large bowl; blend in butter mixture. Spread in a buttered 13"x9" baking pan; press firmly to pack. Bake at 350 degrees until dark and golden, about 20 to 30 minutes; cool for 5 minutes. Break into bite-size pieces; stir in coconut. Store in an airtight container. Makes 1-1/4 pounds.

Fill a gallon-size plastic zipping bag with Brown Sugar Granola and slip inside an old-fashioned oats canister...handy for little ones who like to nibble on the drive to Grandma's house.

Cherry-Hazelnut Clusters

Packed with flavor, this makes a tasty treat for kids who think Thanksgiving dinner will never be ready!

4 1-oz. sqs. white baking
   chocolate, chopped
1 T. shortening
1-1/2 c. chopped hazelnuts,
   toasted

1/2 c. dried tart cherries
12 caramels, unwrapped
2 t. butter

Melt white chocolate with shortening in a heavy saucepan over low heat; stir until melted and smooth. Remove from heat; stir in hazelnuts and cherries. Let cool 10 minutes; drop by teaspoonfuls onto a buttered aluminum foil-lined baking sheet. Set aside to cool. Melt caramels with butter in a heavy, small saucepan; stir until smooth. Drizzle over clusters; set aside until firm. Store in an airtight container. Makes 1-1/2 dozen.

A roomy apothecary jar filled with Cherry-Hazelnut Clusters is a wonderful hostess gift. Dress up the jar by adding a seasonal postcard. Color photocopy the postcard and glue to cardstock. Then, cut the cardstock with decorative-edged scissors, and glue to the front of the jar; let dry.

Chewy Fruit & Nut Bars

Why not get a jump on holiday baking while the family is all together Thanksgiving weekend? It makes for great memories and everyone goes home with treats ready to pop in the freezer for Christmas.

18-oz. can refrigerated sugar
   cookie dough
1 to 2 c. unsalted mixed nuts,
   coarsely chopped

1/2 c. butterscotch chips
1/2 c. mixed dried fruit bits
1/2 c. flaked coconut, toasted

Knead cookie dough until soft; mix in nuts, butterscotch chips and fruit bits. Pat dough into a greased 9"x9" baking pan; sprinkle coconut on top, pressing down lightly with the back of a spoon. Bake at 350 degrees for 30 minutes; cool on a wire rack. Cut into bars; store in an airtight container up to 3 days or in the freezer up to 3 months. Makes about 2-1/2 dozen.

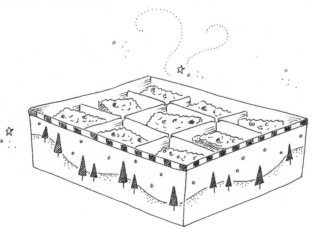

These jewel-toned Chewy Fruit & Nut Bars can be slipped inside a wonderful, vintage Christmas ornament box for gift-giving. Just line the box with wax paper, then store in the freezer until it's time for the annual cookie exchange or visit to a neighbor's home.

October ★ November ★ December

Tasty Topping Seasoning Mix

*Sprinkle over green salads or mashed potatoes...for a quick dip
add 2 tablespoons mix with one cup sour cream!*

2 c. grated Parmesan cheese
1/2 c. sesame seed
1 T. dried, minced onion
1/2 t. dill weed
3 T. celery seed
1/2 t. pepper

1 t. salt
1 t. garlic salt
2 T. dried parsley
2 T. poppy seed
2 t. paprika

Combine ingredients in a one-quart jar; secure lid. Shake to blend;
store in a refrigerator and use within 3 to 4 months. Makes about
3 cups.

Toting the salad to a family get-together? Toss it in a
pretty jadite bowl then sprinkle on some Tasty
Topping Seasoning Mix for everyone to sample. Take
along some extra mix in 1/2-pint jars for
sharing...someone's sure to ask!

Old-Fashioned Sage Stuffing Mix

Once mixed, add any family favorites...sautéed mushrooms, sliced almonds or even minced garlic.

3-1/2 c. unseasoned bread
   cubes
3 T. dried celery
1 T. dried parsley

2 t. dried, minced onion
2 t. chicken bouillon granules
1/2 t. poultry seasoning
1/2 t. dried sage

Place bread cubes in a one-quart, wide-mouth jar; set aside. Spoon remaining ingredients into a small plastic zipping bag; seal. Tuck on top of bread cubes or attach to jar lid. Secure lid; attach instructions.

Instructions:

Bring one cup water, 2 tablespoons butter and seasoning mix packet to a boil; reduce heat and simmer 10 minutes. Remove from heat; set aside. Place jar contents into a large mixing bowl; pour seasoning mixture on top. Mix gently; cover and set aside for 5 minutes. Toss lightly with a fork before serving. Makes 8 serving.

For a hostess gift not soon forgotten, add Old-Fashioned Sage Stuffing Mix to a yellowware bowl, along with some mini pumpkins, sprigs of bittersweet, cinnamon votives and colorful gourds.

October ★ November ★ December

Pilgrim Fudge

Wrap each piece in green, gold or orange-colored cellophane...a bowl full of sweet fall jewels.

3 c. sugar
3/4 c. butter
2/3 c. evaporated milk
1/2 c. canned pumpkin
1/2 t. cinnamon

1/4 t. ground ginger
1/4 t. nutmeg
7-oz. jar marshmallow creme
1 t. vanilla extract
2 c. chocolate chips

Combine first 7 ingredients in a heavy 2-quart saucepan; bring to a boil, stirring constantly. Reduce heat; boil over medium heat until mixture reaches the soft-ball stage, or 234 to 243 degrees on a candy thermometer. Remove from heat; stir in marshmallow creme and vanilla. Fold in chips; blend well. Spread in a buttered 13"x9" baking pan; cool. Cut into squares; store in an airtight container in the refrigerator. Makes about 3-1/2 pounds.

Pumpkin Pie Spice Coffee Creamer

Keep on hand all holiday season to flavor your morning cup of coffee.

4 t. cinnamon
2 t. ground ginger
2 t. nutmeg
1 t. ground cloves

1 t. allspice
1 c. powdered non-dairy
  creamer

Combine ingredients; mix to blend. Store in an airtight container. Makes about 1-1/4 cups.

Pumpkin Pie Squares

An easy switch from traditional pumpkin pie.

1 c. all-purpose flour
1/2 c. quick-cooking oats,
    uncooked
1 c. brown sugar, packed and
    divided
1/2 c. plus 2 T. butter, divided
2 c. canned pumpkin
12-oz. can evaporated milk

2 eggs
3/4 c. sugar
1/2 t. salt
1 t. cinnamon
1/2 t. ground ginger
1/4 t. ground cloves
1/2 c. chopped pecans

Mix flour, oats, 1/2 cup brown sugar and 1/2 cup butter together;
blend until crumbly. Press into the bottom of an ungreased
13"x9" baking pan; bake at 350 degrees for 15 to 20 minutes.
Combine pumpkin, milk, eggs, sugar, salt and spices in a mixing bowl;
pour over crust. Bake 20 additional minutes; toss pecans, remaining
brown sugar and remaining butter together. Sprinkle on top of
pumpkin layer; bake until set, about 15 to 20 minutes. Cool; cut into
squares. Makes 2 dozen.

Pumpkin Pie Squares would look so pretty piled high
in an old-fashioned stoneware bowl. Wrap it all up
with cellophane, gather at the top and tie closed with
raffia and colorful autumn leaves.

159

Light Fruitcake Baked in a Jar

A light-colored fruitcake so the fruits really sparkle!

2 c. chopped pecans
2 c. chopped walnuts
8-oz. pkg. candied red cherries,
    chopped
8-oz. pkg. candied green
    cherries, chopped
1-lb. pkg. candied pineapple,
    chopped
1 c. dates, chopped
1 c. golden raisins
1-3/4 c. all-purpose flour,
    divided

1 c. butter, softened
1 c. sugar
5 eggs
1-1/4 t. baking powder
1 t. salt
1 T. vanilla extract
1 T. orange extract
8 to 10 1-pint, wide-mouth
    canning jars and lids,
    sterilized

Combine nuts and fruit with 1/4 cup flour, tossing to coat; set aside.
Cream butter and sugar until light and fluffy; add eggs, one at a time,
mixing well after each addition. Set aside. Combine remaining flour,
baking powder and salt; blend into sugar mixture. Stir in extracts; fold
in fruit mixture, mixing well. Fill 8 to 10 jars 2/3 full with batter; wipe
rims. Bake at 275 degrees for 40 to 45 minutes; secure with lids and
rings. Set aside to cool; check for seals. Makes 8 to 10 jars.

Once these jars have cooled,
carefully remove the rings,
center a 9-inch length of
ribbon over the lid and place
ring back securely on jar.
Cut a notch in each ribbon
end...simple and festive!

Fruity Freezer Slushes

*Make anytime during the holidays...they keep for up
to a month in the freezer.*

1/2 c. sugar
2 c. water
3 c. unsweetened frozen fruit
    assortment, partially thawed

3/4 c. orange juice
1/4 c. lemon juice

Stir sugar and water together in a one-quart saucepan; heat over
medium heat until mixture boils, stirring until sugar dissolves. Remove
from heat; cool 15 minutes. Purée fruit in a blender; add sugar mixture
and juices, blending until smooth. Divide and pour mixture into
2 freezer-safe 13"x9" baking pans; cover and freeze 8 hours. Break
into small chunks; process in small batches in a food processor until
smooth and slushy. Spoon into a freezer-safe airtight container; cover
and freeze for at least 4 hours. Scoop into cups to serve. Makes
12 servings.

Spoon Fruity Freezer Slushes into tall glasses
decorated with beverage charms! Cut a 6-inch
length of craft wire and using needle-nose
pliers, shape a small loop in one end.
Thread faceted beads and
assorted charms on the wire,
wrap around the glass stem
then twist the end above the
last bead into a loop.

Pineapple Wassail

Bring to a holiday open house while warm...mmmm.

4 c. unsweetened pineapple juice
12-oz. can apricot nectar
2 c. apple cider
1-1/2 c. orange juice

6-inch cinnamon stick, coarsely
  broken
1 t. whole cloves
4 cardamom seeds, crushed

Combine ingredients in a 3-quart saucepan; heat to boiling. Reduce heat and simmer 15 to 20 minutes; strain into serving glasses or punch bowl. Serve warm. Makes about 2 quarts.

Pour Pineapple Wassail into an elegant bottle with a cork, then just copy, cut out and attach this label. What could be easier?

Cranberry Spice Cookies in a Jar

Use sweetened, dried cranberries for the sweet tooth on your gift list.

2 c. all-purpose flour
1/2 t. nutmeg
1/2 t. baking soda
1/8 t. ground cloves
1-1/2 t. cinnamon

2/3 c. dried cranberries
1/2 c. chopped walnuts
2/3 c. brown sugar, packed
1/2 c. sugar

Combine first 5 ingredients together; place in a one-quart, wide-mouth jar, packing firmly. Layer the remaining ingredients in the order listed, packing each layer firmly before adding the next ingredient. Secure lid; attach instructions.

Instructions:

Place mix in a large mixing bowl; gently toss to combine. Mix in one egg, 3/8 cup apple butter, 3 tablespoons melted butter and 1/4 cup buttermilk; blend well. Drop by tablespoonfuls onto greased baking sheets; bake at 375 degrees for 10 to 12 minutes. Cool on baking sheet for one minute; remove to wire rack to cool completely. Makes about 3 dozen.

Wrap a quart jar filled with mix with a 3-inch wide length of corrugated cardboard; glue in place. Add a wide Christmas ribbon on top of cardboard, slightly overlap the ends and glue. Top it all off with red or green raffia tied into a bow...a welcome treat for the office gift exchange!

Fruit-Filled Chocolate Candy

Deliciously different for a neighborhood cookie swap!

9 1-oz. sqs. bittersweet
   chocolate, chopped
2/3 c. mixed dried fruits,
   chopped

1/3 c. mixed nuts, coarsely
   chopped and toasted

Begin by tempering dark chocolate: place 2/3 chocolate in a stainless steel bowl; place over but not touching hot water in a saucepan, stirring until melted. Set chocolate aside to cool to 82 degrees on a candy thermometer; add remaining chopped chocolate, one tablespoon at a time, stirring until melted. The chocolate may be rewarmed immediately by once again placing over hot water and stirring until it reaches 88 degrees. Spoon chocolate into 2-inch disks on a parchment paper-lined baking sheet; sprinkle with fruit and nuts. Set aside until firm, about 15 minutes. Store in an airtight container in a dry, cool cupboard up to 2 weeks. Makes about 2-1/2 dozen.

Slip several candies in these easy to make mugs. Use a white paint pen to draw snowflakes on a blue mug and let dry. Fill with goodies and it's the ideal gift for a favorite snacker!

Cinnamon-Raisin Puffs

Why leave only cookies for Santa...he'll love these buttery treats.

1-1/4 c. milk
1/2 c. egg substitute
1/3 c. sugar
1 t. vanilla extract
1/8 t. salt

1/8 t. nutmeg
4 c. cinnamon-raisin bread, cut
    into 1/2-inch cubes
1 T. butter, melted

Combine first 6 ingredients in a medium mixing bowl; mix well. Add bread cubes; toss until well moistened. Set aside for 15 minutes. Spoon equally into 12 paper-lined muffin cups; drizzle with butter. Bake at 350 degrees until puffed and golden, about 30 to 35 minutes; remove to wire rack to cool completely. Makes one dozen.

Deliver these golden buttery puffs along with a quart of cold milk and a copy of a favorite holiday story to a friend with little ones...what a nice way for them to enjoy some holiday time together.

Date & Nut Muffin Mix

A tasty mix to melt the chills away...be sure to give with a jug of cider for a carefree breakfast.

2 c. self-rising flour
1/2 c. sugar
1/4 c. brown sugar, packed
1 t. cinnamon

1/2 t. nutmeg
1/2 c. chopped pecans
2/3 c. chopped dates

Mix all ingredients except dates together; place in a one-gallon plastic zipping bag. Spoon dates into a small plastic zipping bag; insert into large bag. Seal bags. Attach instructions.

Instructions:

Pour mix into a large mixing bowl; toss in dates, mixing well. Blend in one egg, 3/4 cup milk and 1/4 cup oil; stir until just moistened. Fill greased or paper-lined muffin cups 3/4 full with batter; bake at 400 degrees for 15 to 18 minutes. Makes one dozen.

Roll a festive dinner napkin into a cone shape. Stitch on a big, bright button to help the napkin keep its shape and then slip Date & Nut Muffin Mix inside. Great for drop-in visitors!

Malt Chocolate Waffle Mix

A warm and tasty breakfast mix handy to have waiting in the pantry all Winter long.

1/3 c. powdered malted milk
2-1/2 c. buttermilk biscuit
   baking mix

2 T. sugar
1/3 c. mini chocolate chips

Combine all ingredients in a large plastic zipping bag; seal. Attach instructions.

Instructions:

Place mix in a large mixing bowl; set aside. Blend 2 egg whites until stiff peaks form; set aside. Add 2 egg yolks, 1-1/3 cups buttermilk and 1/2 cup melted butter to mix; blend well. Fold in egg whites; heat according to waffle iron manufacturer's instructions. Makes 6 servings.

This chocolatey waffle mix will delight friends & family! Place it in a simple, homespun covered box, then tie on a set of handmade recipe cards.

Spiced Hot Cocoa Mix

The 1st Day of Winter is December 21st...chase those flurries away
with this warm mix.

1 vanilla bean	3 T. instant espresso
1-1/3 c. sugar	1/2 t. cinnamon
1-1/3 c. powdered milk	1/4 t. vanilla powder
1 c. baking cocoa	1/8 t. ground cardamom

Split vanilla bean; scrape seeds and place in a medium mixing bowl, discarding shell. Add sugar; stir to blend. Add remaining ingredients; mix well. Spoon into an airtight container; attach instructions. Makes about 3-1/2 cups.

Instructions:

Stir 1/4 cup mix into one cup boiling water; stir until dissolved. Makes one serving.

Scoop Spiced Hot Cocoa Mix into a plastic icing bag and fill any extra space at the top with mini marshmallows...what a fun stocking stuffer.

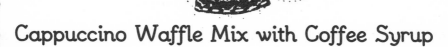

Cappuccino Waffle Mix with Coffee Syrup

Give this mix along with a jar of Coffee Syrup...be sure to keep this gift refrigerated.

1/2 c. butter, softened
1 c. sugar
1-1/2 t. vanilla extract
1-1/3 c. all-purpose flour
1/3 c. powdered milk
1/3 c. powdered non-dairy
    creamer

2 T. instant coffee granules
2 t. baking powder
1/2 t. salt
1/2 t. cinnamon

Cream the first 3 ingredients together in a large mixing bowl; set aside. Combine remaining ingredients; gradually blend into butter mixture until crumbly. Place in a plastic zipping bag. Seal; refrigerate. Tie onto Coffee Syrup container; attach instructions.

Instructions:

Place mix in a mixing bowl; add 3/4 cup water and 2 eggs, stirring until just blended. Bake following waffle iron manufacturer's directions. Serve with warm Coffee Syrup. Makes 5 to 6.

Coffee Syrup:

1 c. brewed coffee   2 c. sugar

Combine both ingredients in a heavy saucepan; stir and heat over medium-high heat until sugar dissolves. Bring to a boil, without stirring; boil for 2 minutes. Remove from heat; cool to room temperature. Store in an airtight container in the refrigerator. Makes 1-3/4 cups.

October ★ November ★ December

Cherry Hot Cocoa Mix

A kid-tested, kid-approved gift mix they can easily make and place in plastic zipping bags all by themselves...have them decorate their own instruction cards.

3/4 c. hot cocoa mix
3/4 t. cherry-flavored drink mix

1/4 c. mini marshmallows
4 cherry licorice whips

Combine first 3 ingredients; place in a plastic zipping bag. Seal. Wrap licorice whips in plastic wrap; tie onto bag. Attach instructions.

Instructions:

Divide mix evenly among 4 mugs; add one cup hot water to each mug. Serve with a licorice whip as a stirrer. Makes 4 servings.

Kids will love finding this yummy cocoa mix inside a whimsical fleece hat!

Trimming-the-Tree Pita Snacks

Add variety…sprinkle with bacon bits, diced pepperoni, dried tomatoes or any other favorite "trimmings."

4 pita rounds
olive oil
1/3 c. grated Parmesan cheese

2 t. dried basil
1/2 t. garlic powder

Carefully split pitas into 2 rounds; slice each round into into 6 wedges. Arrange wedges smooth-side up on aluminum foil-lined baking sheets; brush lightly with olive oil. Flip wedges over; brush with olive oil. Set aside. Combine cheese, basil and garlic powder; sprinkle evenly over wedges. Bake at 350 degrees for 12 to 14 minutes; remove to a wire rack to cool completely. Makes 8 servings.

Share this snack with friends in a snowman basket, it's easy! Glue an orange craft foam nose to the front of a white basket. Add button eyes and a black chenille stem for a smile…don't forget the earmuffs!

Crispy-Crunchy Crouton Sticks

These big dunkers are just right for dips, spreads and even soups.

8-oz. loaf French baguette
1/2 c. butter
1 T. fresh basil, chopped

1/4 t. garlic powder
1/8 t. onion salt

Slice baguette in half horizontally; cut widthwise into one-inch wide sticks. Set aside. Melt butter in a 12" skillet; stir in basil, garlic powder and onion salt. Add half the bread sticks; sauté until coated. Arrange in a single layer in an ungreased jelly-roll pan; repeat with remaining crouton sticks. Bake at 300 degrees for 25 to 30 minutes; flip crouton sticks halfway through baking. Cool completely. Store in an airtight container up to 3 days or freeze up to 3 months. Makes 2 dozen.

Cheery holiday potholders with pockets can be found at any kitchen store. When filled with Crispy-Crunchy Crouton Sticks and a few favorite dip recipes, they're handy keep-on-hand gifts.

Holiday Cheese Ball

Not just any cheese ball...the blend of mascarpone and Gruyère cheeses along with pistachios make this a gourmet delight.

8-oz. carton mascarpone cheese
4-oz. pkg. Gruyère cheese,
   shredded
3 T. pistachios, finely chopped
2 T. fresh basil, chopped

4 t. lemon zest
1/2 t. whole peppercorns,
   coarsely crushed

Blend mascarpone cheese in a medium mixing bowl for 30 seconds with an electric mixer on medium-high setting; add remaining ingredients, mixing well. Pat into a plastic-wrap lined rounded bowl; cover and chill until firm, about 3 hours. Unmold onto a serving platter; remove plastic wrap. Makes 24 servings.

Instead of wrapping a cheese ball in plastic for gift-giving, spoon it into a pretty canning jar with a zinc lid, then tie on a spreader.

October ★ November ★ December

Butterscotch Cut-Outs

*Serve a plate of golden shining stars...simply cut dough out
with all sizes of star-shaped cookie cutters, bake
and decorate with white icing.*

1 c. butterscotch chips, melted
3 c. all-purpose flour
1/2 c. sugar
1/2 c. brown sugar, packed
1 c. butter, softened
1 egg
2 T. milk

1 t. vanilla extract
16-oz. container butter cream
  frosting
Decorations: assorted sanding
  sugars, jimmies and
  sprinkles

Combine melted butterscotch chips with remaining ingredients, except
frosting and decorations, in a large mixing bowl; blend at low speed
with an electric mixer until well mixed, about 2 minutes. Divide
dough in half; wrap each half in plastic wrap and refrigerate until firm,
at least one hour. Roll out dough on a lightly floured surface to
1/8-inch thickness; cut into desired shapes with 2-1/2 inch cookie
cutters. Arrange on parchment paper-lined baking sheets; bake at
375 degrees for 5 to 8 minutes. Cool completely; frost and decorate.
Makes 4 dozen.

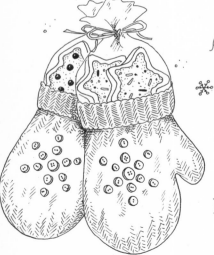

A pair of woolly mittens make
a sweet gift long after the
goodies have been enjoyed.
Stitch white buttons in a
simple snowflake pattern
on a pair of blue mittens
and tuck packaged
Butterscotch Cut-Outs inside.

Gingerbread Cookies in a Jar

Run, run to the cookie jar as fast as you can...there's only one not-eaten gingerbread man!

8 c. all-purpose flour
2 c. sugar
1/4 c. baking powder
1 T. salt
1 T. cinnamon
1 t. baking soda

1 t. ground cloves
1 t. ground ginger
1/2 t. nutmeg
2 c. shortening
4 1-quart, wide-mouth jars and lids

Mix all ingredients except shortening together in a large mixing bowl; cut in shortening with a pastry cutter until coarse crumbs form. Measure 3 cups and spoon into each jar. Secure lids; attach instructions. Use within 3 months. Makes 4 jars.

Instructions:

Place mix in a large mixing bowl; add 1/3 cup molasses, 1/4 cup all-purpose flour and one beaten egg. Blend well; roll out dough on a lightly floured surface to 1/4-inch thickness. Cut into gingerbread shapes using cookie cutters; arrange on greased baking sheets. Bake at 350 degrees for 10 minutes; cool. Makes 2 dozen.

The simplest things can make any gift special. Spray paint a coffee can red, line with homespun and tuck a jar mix inside. Add a wide length of homespun around the middle of the can and knot, then glue a whimsical wooden gingerbread man over the knot.

Christmas Napkin Rings

These could be made for any holiday, just change the fabric...cozy flannel for Winter or colorful oilcloth for Summer.

1/4 yd. fleece or washable felt
tape measure
scissors
4 2-inch diameter mismatched
    buttons

needle & thread
4 hook & loop fasteners

Cut fabric into four, 2"x16" pieces. From one end of a strip, measure in 4 inches and stitch on a decorative button. Turn fabric over and stitch one hook directly on back of the button; repeat with the remaining 3 fabric strips. Turn fabric right-side up, measure in 4 inches from the opposite end where the button is stitched and secure one loop fastener; repeat with remaining 3 lengths of fabric.

To place napkins in napkin rings, center folded napkin on the wrong side of a strip and secure hook & loop fasteners.

These napkin rings can be made from almost anything...mismatched buttons stitched onto elastic or rick-rack, or glittering buttons from an antique shop sewn onto velvet for a more formal get-together.

Christmas Potpourri

Spread a scoop or 2 in a cheery bowl and place beside the fireplace…soon this holiday scent will fill your home.

20 assorted mini pine cones
gold spray paint
3 c. fresh juniper sprigs with
    berries
2 c. red rosebuds
1 c. bay leaves
1/4 c. cinnamon sticks, coarsely
    broken

2 T. whole cloves
10 drops rose essential oil
3 drops pine essential oil
6 drops cinnamon essential oil
1 T. orris root, coarsely chopped
5 whole dried rose blooms
3 3-inch cinnamon sticks

Spray paint pine cones gold; when dry, place in a large ceramic bowl.
Toss with juniper, rosebuds, bay leaves, cinnamon chips and cloves;
set aside. Stir oils and orris root together in a small bowl; drizzle over
pine cone mixture. Toss lightly; place in an airtight container for
2 weeks, shaking daily. Place a couple scoops in a bowl; scatter rose
blooms and cinnamon sticks on top. Makes about 10 cups.

Scoop fragrant Christmas
Potpourri into a tissue-lined wire
stocking. Looks and smells so
fragrant hanging on the mantel.

Festival Fruit Kugel

An easy dish that may be shared warm or cold.

1/2 c. raisins
1/2 c. apple juice
12-oz. pkg. wide egg noodles,
    cooked
1/2 c. margarine

2 apples, cored, peeled and diced
4 eggs, beaten
salt and pepper to taste
cinnamon and sugar to taste

Soak raisins in apple juice overnight; drain and place in a large mixing bowl. Add noodles, margarine and apples; toss to mix. Stir in eggs; season with salt and pepper. Spread in a greased 13"x9" baking pan; sprinkle with cinnamon and sugar. Bake at 375 degrees until top is golden and crisp, about 35 to 45 minutes. Makes 10 servings.

Once cooled, wrap the entire baking pan up in layers of silver tulle tied with white or silver ribbon...a shimmery gift for the holidays.

Potato-Apple Latkes

Celebrate Hanukkah with these traditional pancakes.

4 c. potatoes, baked and
    shredded
1 c. apples, cored, peeled and
    shredded
1/2 c. onion, minced
2 eggs
1/4 c. all-purpose flour

1 t. salt
1/4 t. baking powder
1/4 t. ground coriander
1/8 t. pepper
oil
Garnish: sour cream and honey

Combine all ingredients except oil and garnishes; mix well. Heat
1/4 inch oil in a 10" skillet; drop potato mixture by 1/4 cupfuls into
oil, pressing to flatten slightly. Heat until golden, about 3 minutes; flip
and heat other side until golden. Drain on paper towels; serve warm
with a dollop of sour cream and a drizzling of honey. Makes about
1-1/2 dozen.

Spray paint a paper maché box blue; let dry. Add a
Star of David to the lid using silver paint and when
dry, fill the box with a dreidel and an equal amount
of pennies or chocolate coins...kids love playing this
game! Replace the lid and secure this pretty
packaging with silver ribbon.

S'mores in a Jar

Make lots & lots...there's always room for s'more!

1 sleeve graham crackers,
   crushed
1/3 c. brown sugar, packed

1-1/2 c. mini marshmallows
1 c. milk chocolate chips

Layer ingredients in the order listed in a one-quart, wide-mouth jar. Secure lid; attach instructions.

Instructions:

Pour mix into a greased 9"x9" baking pan; set aside. Whisk 1/2 cup melted butter and 2 teaspoons vanilla extract together; pour over mix. Stir well; pat lightly into pan. Bake at 350 degrees for 15 minutes. Cool; cut into squares. Makes 16.

Just for fun, give S'mores in a Jar along with some chocolate bars, marshmallows and graham crackers for toasting s'mores on a wintry day!

1. Copy
2. Color
3. Cut out
4. Share!

Happy Halloween!

to: from:

to:

from:

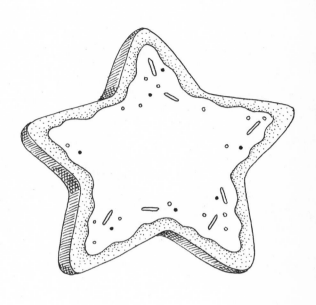

Homemade
Goodies
from:

Every Day Celebrations

★ Every Day Celebrations ★

"Welcome to our Nest!" Treats

It can be hard moving to a new neighborhood where everything is unfamiliar. Help new neighbors feel at ease with a quick visit and these goodies inside a gift basket...you'll be fast friends in no time!

1 c. butterscotch chips	1 t. vanilla extract
1/4 c. corn syrup	3-1/3 c. puffed corn cereal
2 T. milk	1 c. potato sticks
2 T. butter	

Place first 5 ingredients in a heavy saucepan; heat until melted and smooth over low heat, stirring constantly. Remove from heat; stir in remaining ingredients. Drop by rounded tablespoonfuls onto wax paper; set aside until firm. Makes about 3-1/2 dozen.

New neighbors will welcome a cheery housewarming gift basket. Deliver "Welcome to our Nest!" Treats along with a birdhouse, address book and some coupons to any local favorites such as the favorite pizza parlor in town or best carwash.

Home-Sweet-Home Stroganoff Mix

A new home in the same town deserves a new welcome mat, bright shiny house numbers, maybe even a fun mailbox filled with an easy meal mix for those busy unpacking evenings.

2 c. powdered milk
1 c. cornstarch
1/4 c. chicken bouillon granules
3 T. dried, minced onion
1 t. dried basil

1 t. dried thyme
1 t. pepper
2 T. dried parsley
1 T. garlic powder

Combine ingredients; place in an airtight jar or plastic zipping bag. Seal; attach instructions.

Instructions:

Brown one pound ground beef in a 12" skillet; drain. Add 2 cups water, 2 cups uncooked egg noodles and 1/2 cup mix; stir to mix. Bring to a boil; reduce heat and simmer, covered, for 15 to 20 minutes. Top with 1/2 cup sour cream or yogurt; serve warm. Makes 4 servings.

Newlyweds spend lots of time getting unpacked and settled in their new home, so give this mix for a quick meal inside a vintage recipe box along with a few favorite family recipes.

★ Every Day Celebrations ★

Take-a-Break Mocha Muffin Mix

Invite a good friend to come over for coffee...just because.

1-3/4 c. all-purpose flour
3/4 c. plus 1 T. sugar, divided
2 T. plus 1/2 t. baking cocoa,
   divided

2 t. instant coffee granules
2-1/2 t. baking powder
1/2 t. salt
1/2 c. mini chocolate chips

Combine flour, 3/4 cup sugar, 2 tablespoons baking cocoa, coffee, baking powder and salt together. Spoon into a one-quart jar; set aside. Place chocolate chips in a plastic zipping bag; seal and layer on top of mix. Place remaining sugar and remaining cocoa in a mini plastic zipping bag; place into jar. Secure lid; attach instructions.

Instructions:

Combine mix with one cup milk, 1/2 cup melted butter, one beaten egg and one teaspoon vanilla extract; mix until just moistened. Fold in chocolate chips; spoon equally into 12 greased or paper-lined muffin cups. Sprinkle with sugar mixture in small packet; bake at 375 degrees for 15 to 18 minutes. Cool on a wire rack. Makes one dozen.

Tell a best friend no one else can fill her shoes! Cover the lid of a plain box with pictures of shoes cut from magazines or catalogs. Filled with bags of muffin mix and all wrapped up with cotton string, it's a great way to let her know you care.

Good Fortune Honey-Raisin Muffins

A new or first job deserves a celebration!

2 c. all-purpose flour
2 t. baking powder
1 t. ground ginger
1/2 t. nutmeg
1/2 t. allspice
2 eggs, beaten

1/2 c. brown sugar, packed
1/2 c. oil
1/2 c. milk
1/3 c. honey
1 c. raisins

Combine first 5 ingredients in a large mixing bowl; form a well in the center. Set aside. Whisk eggs, brown sugar, oil, milk and honey together; stir into flour mixture until just moistened. Fold in raisins. Spoon into an airtight container; refrigerate up to 3 days. Fill greased or paper-lined muffin cups 2/3 full with batter; bake at 350 degrees for 25 minutes or until a toothpick inserted in the center removes clean. Cool. Makes 14 to 16.

To celebrate a new job, add a shiny penny, some 4-leaf clovers, of course a few memo pads and other fun office supplies nestled in a Chinese take-out box along with Good Fortune Honey-Raisin muffins.

★ Every Day Celebrations

Angelic Ginger Lip Balm

Thank bridesmaids for being such angels! You'll find the ingredients at a health food or craft store.

1 T. almond oil
1 T. jojoba oil
2 t. cocoa butter
2 t. beeswax

1 t. vitamin E oil
4 drops ginger extract
small airtight tin

Heat the first 4 ingredients in a double boiler; stir until melted and smooth. Remove from heat; add remaining ingredients, stirring until almost cool. Pour into a small airtight tin; cool completely. Makes about 2 ounces.

Along with some star-shaped soaps and a heavenly scented candle, a tin of Angelic Ginger Lip Balm can be wrapped up in an antique handkerchief and tied closed with a velvet ribbon.

Brown Sugar-Molasses Bars

A sweet "thank you" for a baby or bridal shower hostess.

1/2 c. butter, softened
1/2 c. brown sugar, packed
1/2 c. molasses
1 egg
1-1/2 c. all-purpose flour
1-1/2 t. baking powder

1 t. ground ginger
1/2 t. salt
1/4 t. baking soda
1/3 c. water
1/2 c. raisins
Garnish: powdered sugar

Cream butter and sugar until light and fluffy; blend in molasses and egg. Set aside. Combine flour, baking powder, ginger, salt and baking soda; mix into creamed mixture alternately with water. Fold in raisins; spread into a greased 13"x9" baking pan. Bake at 350 degrees 20 to 25 minutes; cool and sprinkle with powdered sugar. Cut into bars to serve. Makes 3 dozen.

Cut these Brown Sugar-Molasses Bars with a heart-shaped cookie cutter, then place in an old hatbox tied up with soft tulle...sure to get smiles!

★ Every Day Celebrations

Best-Friend Brownies

We can all use a boost now & then, and nothing does it like chocolate!

2 c. chocolate chips
1 c. evaporated milk
3 c. vanilla wafers, crushed

2 c. mini marshmallows
1 c. powdered sugar

Combine first 2 ingredients in a saucepan; heat over low heat until melted and smooth; set aside 1/2 cup mixture, pour remaining mixture into a large mixing bowl. Stir in vanilla wafer crumbs, mini marshmallows and powdered sugar; spread into a buttered 8"x8" baking pan, pressing down gently. Spread with reserved chocolate mixture; refrigerate one hour. Slice into squares to serve. Makes about 1-1/2 dozen.

Tie on a gift tag with this quote:

There's nothing better than a good friend, except a good friend with chocolate.
-Linda Grayson

Giant Cookies for a True-Blue Friend

Brighten a friend's day by telling her how special she is.

1 c. graham cracker crumbs
2/3 c. all-purpose flour
1/2 t. baking soda
1/4 t. salt
1/2 c. butter

2/3 c. sugar
1 egg
1 t. vanilla extract
2/3 c. chocolate chips

Combine first 4 ingredients in a medium mixing bowl; set aside. Cream butter and sugar until light and fluffy; blend in egg and vanilla. Gradually mix in flour mixture; mix well. Drop by 1/4 cupfuls onto ungreased baking sheets; flatten slightly with the back of a wooden spoon. Sprinkle chocolate chips evenly over the tops; lightly press into dough. Bake at 325 degrees for 15 to 20 minutes. Makes about one dozen.

A true-blue basket of niceties...blue washcloths, a big blue fluffy towel, some fuzzy blue slippers and a big bag of these chocolatey cookies.

★ Every Day Celebrations

Birthday Bash in a Bag

Turning a year older can be fun when you give this birthday bag filled with everything needed for a day of fun!

sweet treats
shoe box lid
colorful cellophane
candles
large gift bag

assorted colors curling ribbon
party supplies such as hats,
  noisemakers, balloons,
  plates, napkins, confetti
gift tag

Place treats inside shoe box lid, wrap with cellophane, gathering edges at the top. Secure with lengths of curling ribbon. Set inside gift bag. Fill bag with party supplies, blowing up some balloons to tuck inside as well. Glue strands of curling ribbon inside a party hat; curl the ends. Glue hat to the top of the gift bag along with a noisemaker. Tie on gift tag that reads "Birthday Bash in a Bag!"

This party idea can be used for any special celebration...anniversaries, graduations, promotions or surprise showers!

"Today is Your Birthday!" Cakes

A tiny tiered treasure for the birthday girl!

18-1/2 oz. pkg. white cake mix
1-1/4 c. water
3 eggs
2 T. oil

1 t. vanilla extract
1/2 t. coconut extract
Garnish: strawberry slices,
    chocolate curls, jimmies

Blend first 4 ingredients together; add extracts, mixing well. Spread into a greased and floured jelly-roll pan; bake at 350 degrees until a toothpick inserted in the center removes clean, about 20 minutes. Cool completely. Cut five, 3-inch round circles, 2-inch round circles and one-inch round circles out of cake. Place each of the larger layers on its own plate; frost. Stack 2-inch layers on top; frost. Add smallest layer; frost. Decorate with desired garnishes. Makes 5 cakes.

Creamy Frosting:

3 T. all-purpose flour
1 c. milk
1 c. butter, softened

1 c. powdered sugar
1 t. vanilla extract

Combine flour and milk in a medium saucepan; stir over low heat until thickened. Remove from heat; cool. Cream butter in a large mixing bowl; add powdered sugar, blending until fluffy. Mix in vanilla; add flour mixture, blending until thick and smooth.

They'll jump for joy! Tie up guests' party favor bags
with curling ribbon and a jump rope
for take-home fun!

★ Every Day Celebrations ★

"What a Great Catch!" Snack Mix

Let that special guy know how you feel!

2 qts. popped popcorn
8 c. bite-size crispy corn cereal
   squares
4 c. corn chips
2 c. fish-shaped bite-size
   Cheddar cheese crackers

3 T. butter, melted
1 t. chili powder
1/3 c. grated Parmesan cheese
1/4 c. bacon bits

Combine first 4 ingredients in a large bowl; set aside. Heat remaining ingredients together in a small saucepan until butter is melted; drizzle over popcorn mix. Toss to coat evenly. Makes about 5 quarts.

Fill a fishbowl with these snacks, tie on a bobber
or 2 and let him know he's quite a catch!

"Happy Anniversary!" Scones in a Jar

Make it a special breakfast for a special day.

1-3/4 c. all-purpose flour
1 T. baking powder
1/2 t. salt
1 c. quick-cooking oats,
    uncooked

1/2 c. chopped pecans
1/2 c. mini chocolate chips

Combine first 3 ingredients; layer into a one-quart, wide-mouth jar; pack firmly. Layer remaining ingredients on top; secure lid. Attach instructions.

Instructions:

Place mix in a medium mixing bowl; cut in one cup sliced butter with a pastry cutter until coarse crumbs form. Set aside. Whisk 1/3 cup honey, 1/4 cup milk and one egg together; add to dry ingredients, mixing until just moistened. Knead on a lightly floured surface 8 to 10 times; pat into an 8-inch circle. Slice into 8 wedges; arrange one inch apart on an ungreased baking sheet. Bake at 375 degrees for 10 to 12 minutes. Makes 8 servings.

Give an apron with this scone mix...don't forget to slip sample-size jars of tasty jams and jellies in the apron pockets.

★ Every Day Celebrations

"Hey, Sports Fan!" Sweet Pretzel Batch

Celebrate those big wins in high school and college sports games!

3/4 c. butter
3/4 c. sugar
1/8 t. nutmeg
1 egg

2 c. all-purpose flour
1/2 c. pistachios, finely chopped
    and divided

Cream butter; add sugar and nutmeg. Blend in egg and flour; fold in 1/4 cup pistachios. Form dough by single tablespoonfuls into circles, X's, rods or pretzel shapes; arrange one inch apart on ungreased baking sheets. Bake at 375 degrees for 6 to 8 minutes; transfer to a wire rack placed over wax paper. Brush with glaze; sprinkle with remaining pistachios. Makes about 3 dozen.

Glaze:

1 c. powdered sugar
1 t. vanilla extract

1 to 2 T. milk

Whisk ingredients together until desired glaze consistency is achieved.

Shape a new deflated basketball, football or soccer ball into a bowl and fill to the rim with these pretzels and other snacks.

GO TEAM!

Away-Game Snack Mix

A spicy munchie to take anywhere.

1 t. chili powder
1/2 t. onion powder
1/2 t. garlic powder
1/2 t. coarse salt
1/8 t. cayenne pepper

2 qts. popped popcorn
2 c. mini pretzels
2 c. bite-size corn cereal
    squares, toasted

Combine first 5 ingredients together; set aside. Gently toss popcorn, pretzels and cereal together in a large mixing bowl; sprinkle with seasonings. Toss again; store in an airtight container. Makes 12 servings.

Pour Away-Game Snack Mix into easy-to-tote sports bottles that can be used again and again.

★ Every Day Celebrations

Get-Well-Wishes Soup Mix

Everyone needs a little TLC when they're feeling under the weather.

1/4 c. red lentils
2 T. dried onion flakes
2-1/2 t. chicken bouillon
    granules
1 c. egg noodles

1/8 t. celery seed
1/8 t. garlic powder
1/2 t. dill weed
1 bay leaf

Layer all ingredients in a 2-cup, wide-mouth jar in the order listed. Seal jar tightly.

Instructions:

Bring 8 cups water to a boil in a large saucepan; add soup mix. Cover and simmer 25 minutes. Remove bay leaf and stir in 1-1/2 cups frozen corn and 2 cups cooked, diced chicken. Simmer 5 minutes or until heated through. Makes 8 servings.

Remember all the nice things that go along with making someone feel better...crossword puzzles, a book by a favorite author, a box of tissues and a hot water bottle.

P.B. & J. Cookies

*Little ones need extra hugs & kisses when they're not feeling well so
serve these cookies with a glass of milk using an old chalkboard
as a tray. Include a tin of colored chalk just for fun.*

1/2 c. butter, softened
1/2 c. creamy peanut butter
1 c. brown sugar, packed
1 egg
1 t. vanilla extract
1-1/2 c. all-purpose flour

1/2 t. baking soda
1/2 t. baking powder
1/4 t. salt
1/3 c. chopped peanuts
1/2 c. grape jelly

Cream butter, peanut butter and sugar together; blend in egg and
vanilla until fluffy. Set aside. Combine flour, baking soda, baking
powder and salt; gradually mix into peanut butter mixture. Fold in
peanuts; mix well. Roll into one-inch balls; arrange on lightly greased
baking sheets. Make an indentation in the center of each ball with
the back of a spoon; fill with jelly. Bake at 350 degrees for 10 to
12 minutes. Makes about 3-1/2 dozen.

Give 'em a bucket of
fun! Fill a bright tin
pail with these
cookies and some
new crayons,
coloring books,
puzzles and markers.

★ Every Day Celebrations

Boatloads-of-Fun Cookies in a Jar

For a friend taking a vacation...great for nibbling on the road!

1-3/4 c. white cake mix   1 T. sugar
1/2 c. gumdrops, halved

Spoon cake mix into a one-quart, wide-mouth jar; set aside. Toss gumdrops and sugar together; layer on top of cake mix. Secure lid; attach instructions.

Instructions:

Place mix in a medium mixing bowl; add one egg white and 1/4 cup oil. Mix well; shape into one-inch balls. Arrange 2 inches apart on greased baking sheets; bake at 350 degrees until golden, about 12 to 15 minutes. Makes 1-1/2 dozen.

Mix up a batch of cookies ahead of time and give, along with the jar mix, inside a toy bathtime boat. Don't forget to add playing cards, travel-size games, drawing pads, washable crayons and short reading...all things that keep kids entertained on the drive!

Travelin' Snacks

Let a friend who's moving away know you'll miss her.

2 c. mini pretzel twists
2 c. doughnut-shaped oat cereal
2 c. bite-size crispy rice cereal
   squares
2 c. fruit-flavored corn puff
   cereal
2 c. wheat puff cereal
2 c. toasted croutons
2 c. bite-size Cheddar cheese
   cracker squares

2 c. assorted nuts
1/2 c. butter
1 c. brown sugar, packed
1/4 c. corn syrup
1/2 t. salt
1/2 t. vanilla extract
1/2 t. baking soda
1 c. raisins

Combine first 8 ingredients in a large roaster; set aside. Heat butter, brown sugar, corn syrup and salt over medium heat; bring to a boil, stirring constantly. Boil for 5 minutes without stirring; remove from heat. Add vanilla and baking soda; pour over mix, stirring until coated. Bake at 275 degrees for one hour, stirring every 15 minutes; mix in raisins. Spread on buttered aluminum foil to cool. Store in an airtight container. Makes 16 cups.

For a clever container, use spray adhesive to cover a new, one-gallon paint can with a map. Then fill the can with a travel journal, address book, notepad, pens, disposable camera, stamps, envelopes and a bag of Travelin' Snacks.

Happy Trails!

It's-a-Sleepover Late Night Snack

Tasty homemade pizza is the favorite food for a girls' sleepover!

10-oz. pkg. refrigerated pizza
    dough
1/2 c. pizza sauce, divided

18 slices pepperoni
6 mozzarella cheese sticks

Roll out pizza dough into a 12"x9" rectangle; slice into six, 4-1/2"x4" strips. Spread one tablespoon pizza sauce down the center third of each strip; top with 3 pepperoni slices and one mozzarella cheese stick. Fold dough over cheese stick; pinch dough seams to seal. Arrange seam-side down on a greased baking sheet; bake at 425 degrees until golden, about 10 minutes. Makes 6 servings.

Give the girls a little make-up kit with glittery nail polish, hair clips, flavored lip gloss, hair scrunchies, lotions and powders...plenty to keep them busy while the pizza's baking.

S'more Kit

After pizza, the girls will want a sweet treat.

2 bananas
2 2-1/4 oz. milk chocolate
   candy bars

7-oz. jar marshmallow creme
1 box graham crackers

Pack all ingredients safely in a sturdy box; add instructions. Seal and deliver.

Instructions:

Peel and slice bananas; set aside. Break chocolate into squares; set aside. Run marshmallow creme jar under hot water until soft; wipe off and set aside. Break one sleeve graham crackers into squares; spread marshmallow creme on 2 squares. Place one chocolate square on one graham cracker; top with 2 or 3 slices banana. Top with remaining graham cracker, creme-side down; squish gently. Repeat with remaining ingredients. Makes 8.

Wrap up all the fixin's for this kit with an old-fashioned thriller movie...a perfect late-night match!

★ Every Day Celebrations

Twinkle Toes

For a mom that's on her feet all day, put together a reviving foot spa...she'll definitely thank you!

1 pt. boiling water	2 T. sea salt
6 T. fresh mint, chopped	2 drops lavender essential oil

Pour boiling water over the mint leaves; let steep 8 minutes. Strain and add sea salt; let cool. Add lavender oil. Pour into a pint jar with a tight-fitting lid. Makes one bath.

Along with a bottle of Twinkle Toes, add a bag filled with smooth pebbles, an exfoliating cloth and fluffy towel. Tie on these instructions: For a gentle foot massage, place pebbles in a shallow bowl and cover with warm water. Add bottle of Twinkle Toes then rub feet over pebbles.

Crunchy Fudge

Fudge is always an indulgence...just what every new mom needs!

4 c. sugar	6 T. butter
1 c. evaporated milk	1 t. vanilla extract
1/2 c. corn syrup	

Combine sugar, evaporated milk, corn syrup and butter in a heavy saucepan; heat over medium-low heat until sugar dissolves. Increase heat to medium; heat to boiling, stirring occasionally. Heat, without stirring, to the soft-ball stage, or 234 to 240 degrees on a candy thermometer; remove from heat. Place pan in a 1-1/2 inch deep cold water bath; add vanilla, without stirring. Let cool to 110 degrees; remove from water bath. Blend until fudge thickens and loses its gloss; spread evenly in 2 buttered 8"x8" baking pans. Pour topping on top; let cool. Cut into squares to serve. Makes 3-1/3 pounds.

Topping:

1 c. sugar	2 T. evaporated milk
1/4 c. water	1 t. vanilla extract
1/4 c. butter	1 c. chopped pecans, toasted

Stir sugar and water together in a small skillet; heat over medium-high heat until sugar dissolves. Increase heat to high; stir until mixture turns golden. Remove from heat; carefully add butter, evaporated milk and vanilla, stirring to mix. Add pecans; stir to coat.

Give Mom just what she needs to get started scrapbooking...a baby album, decorative-edged scissors, pretty papers, stickers, beads and tags so everything will be at her fingertips!

"Oops!" Apple Pie

Say "I'm sorry" with an upside-down apple pie.

1/2 c. walnut halves
1/3 c. brown sugar, packed
1 c. sugar
2 T. all-purpose flour
1/2 t. cinnamon

2 t. plus 1/8 t. salt
1 T. lemon juice
5 c. apples, cored, peeled and
    sliced
9-inch pie crust

Arrange walnut halves, round-side down on the bottom of a greased 9-inch springform baking pan; sprinkle with brown sugar. Set aside. Combine sugar, flour, cinnamon, 1/8 teaspoon salt and lemon juice; mix well. Stir in apples; spread over walnut mixture. Carefully place pie crust on top of apple mixture; fold under and flute to form a rim. Vent crust; place in an aluminum foil-lined jelly-roll pan. Bake at 350 degrees until apples are tender, about 55 minutes. Carefully, invert onto a serving plate; remove form. Makes 8 servings.

Sometimes things
get
topsy-turvy.

After wrapping up "Oops!" Apple Pie, tie this tag on.

Ooey-Gooey Brownie Bars

Sometimes we all need a little encouragement.

1/2 c. shortening	1 t. vanilla extract
1-1/4 c. sugar	1 c. all-purpose flour
2 eggs	1 t. baking powder
1/2 c. applesauce	1/2 t. salt
1/4 c. chocolate chips	1/2 t. cinnamon

Cream shortening and sugar; blend in eggs. Add applesauce, chocolate chips and vanilla; mix well and set aside. Combine remaining ingredients; stir into creamed mixture. Spread in a greased 13"x9" baking pan. Bake at 350 degrees for 25 minutes; let cool slightly. Drizzle with glaze; let cool completely. Slice into bars to serve. Makes 3 dozen.

Glaze:

3/4 c. powdered sugar	milk
1/8 t. cinnamon	

Toss powdered sugar and cinnamon together; stir in enough milk to reach desired drizzling consistency.

Fill a cowboy hat with wrapped brownie bars and a sheriff's badge tag that reads "Hang in the saddle!"

Sweet 16 Bars

These ginger & spice cookies tell her she's everything nice!

1/4 c. butter, softened	1 t. baking soda
1 c. sugar	1/2 t. cinnamon
3/4 c. creamy peanut butter	1/4 t. nutmeg
1 egg	1/8 t. ground ginger
1-1/4 c. all-purpose flour	1 c. applesauce

Cream butter in a large mixing bowl; gradually blend in sugar, peanut butter and egg. Set aside. Combine flour, baking soda, cinnamon, nutmeg and ginger; add alternately with applesauce to the peanut butter mixture. Spread batter into a greased 8"x8" baking pan; bake at 350 degrees until a toothpick inserted in the center removes clean, about 40 minutes. Cool; cut into squares. Makes 16.

Wrapped up and tucked inside a jewelry box along with a sentimental piece of jewelry these make a special Sweet 16 gift. Pass along a favorite locket, charm bracelet or other handed-down keepsake.

Chip, Chip, Hooray Cookies

Say "Congrats!" to the new driver!

3/4 c. sugar
3/4 c. brown sugar, packed
1 c. butter, sliced
2 eggs
1 t. vanilla extract

2-1/4 c. all-purpose flour
1 t. baking soda
1 c. pecan pieces
2 c. chocolate chips

Combine first 5 ingredients in a food processor; process until creamy. Add flour and baking soda; process until just combined. Fold in pecans and chocolate chips; drop by rounded teaspoonfuls 2 inches apart on ungreased baking sheets. Bake at 375 degrees for 8 to 10 minutes. Makes about 4 dozen.

A tall plastic pail filled with car washing supplies...paper towels, window and upholstery cleaner, sponges, a pair of fuzzy dice and these yummy cookies will make any new driver feel like hitting the open road!

★ Every Day Celebrations ★

Fiesta Refried Bean Mix

A fun-filled college student care package.

3 c. dried pinto beans
1 T. cumin
1 T. chili powder

1 t. salt
1 t. pepper
3 T. dried, minced onion

Grind beans to a flour consistency in a coffee grinder, food mill or blender; add remaining ingredients. Spoon into a plastic zipping bag; seal. Attach instructions.

Instructions:

Place 3/4 cup mix in a saucepan with 2-1/2 cups boiling water; whisk to combine. Bring mixture to a boil; reduce heat and simmer 4 to 5 minutes or until desired consistency is reached. Serves 4.

A bag of tortilla chips, jar of salsa, some brightly colored lanterns, paper flowers and maracas make a complete fiesta for sharing with roommates!

Italian Pizza Mix

Another fun care package idea!

1-1/2 c. bread flour
1 c. whole-wheat flour

1/2 t. salt
1 pkg. active dry yeast

Combine flours and salt in a plastic zipping bag; seal. Attach yeast envelope and instructions.

Instructions:

Sprinkle yeast over one cup 105 to 115-degree water in a medium mixing bowl; set aside until foamy, about 5 minutes. Add mix and 2 tablespoons oil; stir vigorously for 20 strokes. Set aside for 20 minutes. Divide dough in half; spread each half into a 12" pizza pan that has been greased and then sprinkled with cornmeal. Bake at 425 degrees until golden, about 10 minutes. Sprinkle with 1/2 cup shredded mozzarella cheese, an 8-ounce can pizza sauce and any favorite toppings. Sprinkle with additional cheese; bake 10 additional minutes or until cheese is bubbly. Makes 16 servings.

Wrap up Italian Pizza Mix in a red & white checked tablecloth...add some toppings and pizza sauce and place it all in a big white chef's hat.

Rosemary Foccaccia Mix

Congratulate the groom-to-be!

1 pkg. active dry yeast	1-1/2 t. dried rosemary
1 T. sugar	1-1/2 c. bread flour
2 t. red pepper flakes	1/2 t. salt

Combine ingredients; place in an airtight container. Seal; attach instructions.

Instructions:

Place mix in a large mixing bowl; add 1/2 cup very warm water and 2 tablespoons olive oil. Stir with a wooden spoon until smooth; knead 8 to 10 times. Place in a greased bowl, turning to coat all sides; cover and let rise until double in bulk. Punch dough down; roll out on a greased jelly-roll pan into a 13"x9" rectangle; brush with 2 tablespoons olive oil. Sprinkle with coarse salt to taste; bake at 425 degrees for 5 minutes. Pop any bubbles with a fork; bake 8 additional minutes. Remove from pan; cut into 3-inch squares. Makes about 12 servings.

Rosemary Foccaccia Mix paired with a jar of pesto sauce and bottle of sparkling cider make a terrific presentation when given in a top hat!

Honey Spice Cookies in a Jar

Let the bride-to-be know she's found a honey of a guy!

2-3/4 c. all-purpose flour
1 T. ground ginger
2 t. cinnamon
1 t. baking soda
1 t. salt

1/4 t. ground cloves
1/4 t. nutmeg
1/2 t. vanilla powder
1-1/2 c. quick-cooking oats,
    uncooked

Layer ingredients in the order listed in a one-quart, wide-mouth jar; pack firmly. Secure lid; attach instructions.

Instructions:

Place mix in a large mixing bowl; gently toss. Add one cup softened butter, 3/4 cup honey and one egg; mix well. Cover and refrigerate overnight. Shape into one-inch balls; flatten slightly with the bottom of a cup dipped in sugar. Arrange on ungreased baking sheets; bake at 350 degrees until golden, about 5 to 8 minutes. Makes about 6 dozen.

Send along best wedding wishes by wrapping this jar mix in several layers of tulle and tying with a length of silk ribbon.

Best Wishes

Thinking-of-You Turtle Candies

A sweet way to let someone know they're missed.

36 mini baking cups
6 1-oz. sqs. bittersweet baking
   chocolate, chopped and
   melted

2-1/4 oz. pkg. pecan pieces,
   divided
6-oz. pkg. caramels, unwrapped
1 to 2 T. water

Arrange baking cups in a jelly-roll pan; set aside. Place 1/2 teaspoon chocolate in the center of each baking cup; sprinkle each with a few pecan pieces. Set aside until firm. Melt caramels over a double boiler, adding one to 2 tablespoons water to thin; cool slightly. Spoon 1/4 teaspoon over pecan pieces; set aside to harden. Top each with 1/2 teaspoon melted chocolate; set aside until firm. Drizzle with remaining melted caramel; set aside until firm. Makes 3 dozen.

For an invitation to chat any time, tuck a phone card into a gift box filled with these turtle candies.

Nutty Ginger Rice Mix

Sometimes a thoughtful note is the best way to keep in touch.
This cinnamony rice mix will be a sweet addition tucked into a
gift box with card-making supplies.

1 c. long-grain rice, uncooked
1/2 c. roasted peanuts
1 t. cinnamon

1 t. ground ginger
1 cube chicken bouillon,
    crumbled

Combine ingredients; place in an airtight container. Seal;
attach instructions.

Instructions:

Bring 1/4 cup butter, 1/4 cup honey and 2 cups water to a boil in a
saucepan; reduce heat. Add rice mix; simmer 20 minutes. Makes
6 servings.

Fill a mini box with all the essentials for making
handmade cards...scraps of vintage floral fabrics,
buttons, colorful card stock, ribbon, a glue stick,
envelopes and stamps. Tie up this pretty package
with a ribbon threaded through a decorative
buckle or brooch.

★ Every Day Celebrations

Country Herb Dip Mix

Invite out-of-town friends for a long weekend and spend time checking out antique shops, the farmers' market and local auctions together.

1 T. dried chives
1 t. garlic salt
1/2 t. dill weed

1/2 t. paprika
1/8 t. onion powder

Combine ingredients in a small bowl; spoon into the center of a 6-inch square of aluminum foil. Fold to seal; use within 6 months. Attach instructions.

Instructions:

Combine mix with one tablespoon lemon juice, one cup mayonnaise and one cup sour cream. Refrigerate until chilled. Makes 2 cups.

As friends are packing to head back home, send along a little reminder of their weekend in the country...set a garden trug with this mix and fresh veggies from the garden in their back seat.

Patio Pals Onion-Cheese Dip Mix

Sometimes spur-of-the-moment gatherings turn out to be the most fun! Give a quick call to the neighbors, whip up this dip, chop some veggies and then spend time catching up.

1 T. dried, minced onion
1/2 t. beef bouillon granules
1 T. grated Parmesan cheese

1/4 t. garlic salt
1/8 t. white pepper

Mix ingredients together; spoon into the center of a 6-inch square of aluminum foil. Fold to seal; use within 6 months. Attach instructions.

Instructions:

Combine mix with one cup sour cream; refrigerate until chilled. Makes one cup.

Patio chats can last well into the evening, so set out twinkling votives nestled inside colorful retro drinking glasses. Add some sea salt crystals inside the glasses...they'll steady the votives and add sparkle.

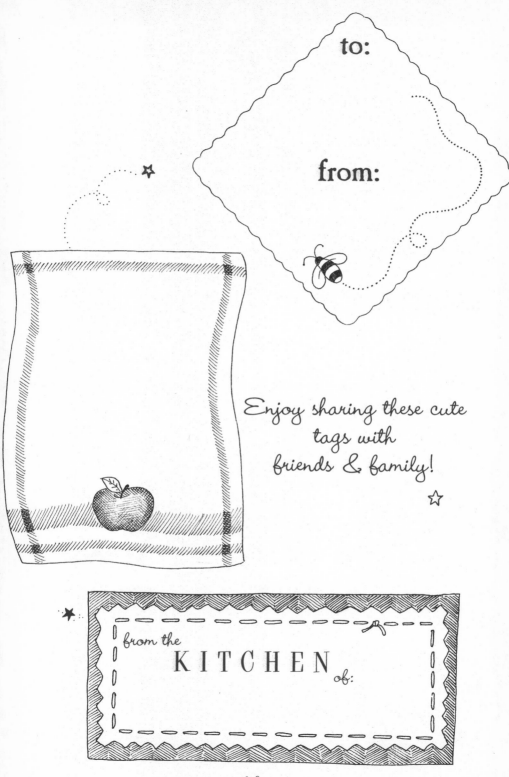

to:

from:

Enjoy sharing these cute
tags with
friends & family!

from the
KITCHEN of:

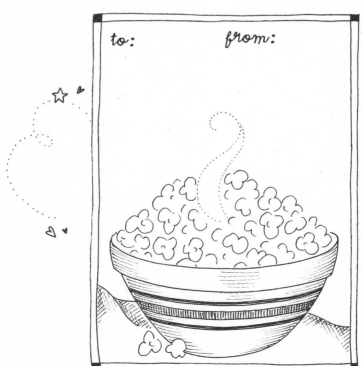

to: from:

Index

Index

Index